My Child Wasn't Born Perfect

My Child Wasn't Born Perfect

Learning Disabilities and Autism,
The Quest and Success of a Child

Kimberly Bell Mocini

PRINCIPIA
MEDIA

My Child Wasn't Born Perfect
© 2012 Kimberly Mocini
Published by Principia Media, LLC, Wyoming, MI
www. principiamedia.com

ISBN-13: 978-161485-303-5

Disclaimer: Certain names, identifying details and events have been changed to protect the privacy of individuals. The author has faithfully tried to recreate events, locales and conversations often from memory. Although the author and publisher have made every effort to ensure that the information in this book is correct, the author and publisher do not assume and hereby disclaim any liability to any party for any loss, damage, or disruption caused by errors or omissions, whether such errors or omissions result from negligence, accident, or other cause. The book is not intended as a substitute for the medical advice of physicians, mental health or other professionals, including teachers and administrators. Readers are urged to consult with trained professionals before determining a course of treatment for those with autism and/or learning disabilities.

Printed in the United States of America

18 17 16 15 14 13 12   7 6 5 4 3 2 1

Cover Design: Frank Gutbrod
Interior Layout: Virginia McFadden

DEDICATION

This book is dedicated to my mother, Jean, who has supported me in numerous ways throughout my life; to my stepson, Jimmy, and his family, as they grow with each new experience; to my husband, David, as your love brightens each and every day; and to my children, DJ, Jeffrey, and Jayson, you are the treasures I hold close to my heart.

ACKNOWLEDGMENTS

I would like to begin by thanking my publisher, Principia Media and Dirk Wierenga, for giving me direction in bringing this book to print. A thank you to my aunt, Margaret Badoud Thompson, who suggested in the early days that I have my son tested. Words cannot express the gratitude to Deb Munson, who taught me how to help my child and to Margaret Spyker, who brought me the term, Hyperlexia. I would like to acknowledge the many teachers and support staff in the Saugatuck School system who gave so much of their time and energy to my children, my husband and me. Also, a heartfelt thank you goes to Tom Clark and Dan Wilson, who helped in so many ways throughout the middle school and high school years.

A special thank you goes to Shelley Scholten, not only for her expertise in speech pathology but all her efforts in organizing a special network within the school system to assist my child. Too numerous to mention are the extraordinary tasks she did behind the scenes that made such a difference in my child's education. Shelley's passion and commitment to the special children blessed with learning disabilities goes far beyond the rest. I will be forever grateful.

CONTENTS

Foreword
viii

Introduction
xi

Afterword—JD's Comments
111

About the Author
116

FOREWORD

My Child Wasn't Born Perfect is a story of the journey of JD from early childhood to young adulthood, as told through his mother's eyes and voice. JD's mother shares the struggles of educating a child with language and social challenges in the 1990s when there was limited knowledge of Hyperlexia (the ability to read before his peers) or Autism Spectrum Disorders. All she knew was that JD learned differently, and that she had to be his advocate.

This story chronicles JD's educational interventions and experiences. Mrs. Mocini sought out private resources and public resources to help her son be the best that he could be. Having been a part of this journey with JD, I have had the pleasure of watching JD grow and develop. At the onset of JD's education, he was considerably behind his peers in his language skills. By working with JD's "gifts" of a strong visual memory and Hyperlexia, the educators found they could help JD grow in his expressive and receptive language skills. Through the help of private and school speech-language therapy, accommodations in the general education setting, and a lot of work at home, JD's language skills began to flourish.

Many of the "new and unique" accommodations and strategies used with JD in the 1990s are still used today in most educational settings. Today, however, these accommodations are no longer unique but are commonplace. Nearly every elementary teacher has a visual daily schedule, accommodates for sensory needs, teaches to children's varying learning styles (visual, auditory, tactile), and communicates regularly with parents. These accommodations are typically provided without an IEP (Individualized Educational Plan/Program), however, some children still need additional supports for learning that require an IEP.

Once JD's language skills began to improve in elementary school, the journey was not over for JD or his family. In fact, the journey just took a new turn to the social arena. Although never officially diagnosed, it was beginning to look like JD may have an Autism Spectrum Disorder (ASD). The CDC (Centers for Disease Control & Prevention) reports that an average of 1 in 110 children in the United States have an ASD. Likewise, an ASD is four to five times more likely to occur in boys than in girls (www. cdc.gov/ncbddd/autism/data.html).

Given JD's "gifts" of a near photographic memory, high intellect, and honesty, there were many talents that could take JD far in life, but he first had to survive the teen years. JD's mother shares many stories of the social challenges her son encountered. Some will bring you to tears, but these stories need to be heard. Parents and educators need to keep their eyes and ears open. It is a "wake-up call" for everyone. Bullying can be bold or subtle, but must not be tolerated in any setting.

Throughout this book, JD's mother reveals the highs and lows of raising a child who learns differently. This book could be of benefit to any reader, for don't we all know someone with a disability? The CDC reports that, "Approximately 13 percent of children have a developmental disability, ranging from mild disabilities such as speech and language impairments to serious developmental disabilities, such as intellectual disabilities, cerebral palsy, and autism" (www.cdc.gov/ncbddd/autism/data.html). Statistics say that there is a rise in identification of ASD, ADHD, and a variety of other disabilities. This could be true, or it could be that we just know more than we knew 20 years ago. Does it really matter? What matters is what we do. How we parent, how we educate, and how we all work together to help a child be the best that he or she can be. This is what truly matters, not statistics. This was the goal of JD's mother, and it is shared time and time again throughout the story of JD.

JD's story is a success story. A combination over time of many approaches and many people working together with JD, helping him be the best that he could be. Likewise, JD had a mother and a family who never gave up, and always believed in him. Their love and support was unfailing. Most of the words in this book are from JD's mother and through her eyes, but the final words in this book are from JD. What wonderful words from a young man who has lived with and learned from his disability. Words of understanding and hope for all!

Shelley Scholten,
Speech-Language Pathologist
Saugatuck Schools

INTRODUCTION

Much of what I have written about in this book is from my own experiences and perspective as a parent of a child with a learning disability—or should I say learning disorder. The reason for sharing the story of my son is the hope that one suggestion, thought, or ounce of encouragement will help another child, parent, day care provider, teacher, family or anyone that might play a part in the life of a child born with a learning disability or learning disorder—a child that wasn't born perfect.

Let me start by saying that I am not a therapist or a specialist. Rather, I am the mother of three wonderful boys, with a terrific husband, who happens to be blessed with a child born with a learning disorder. In addition I have a college education and have been in the business world for thirty-plus years. As is the case with many families today, I have had to work outside the home while raising my family. Our family is just like so many others. We have had our ups and downs and challenges in life. There have been job loss and family tragedies. As a family we have not been spared any of the normal day-to-day or year-to-year challenges we face in the world today.

After the birth of my first child, I remember asking the doctor for an instruction manual as I had never before changed a diaper or babysat younger children, and I surely did not know what to do with this new baby. Little did I know that my second child would be more of a challenge than the first. Making it more complicated was a third child, and mixing in a stepson who came to live with us.

Though I could not predict the future then and still do not have all the answers today, there is one thing that I do know. I know that I made a difference in the outcome of my son's life. Because of my own experience, I know in my heart that you, too, can make a difference. Just be ready and willing to give it your all, because it will not be easy. There will be times of despair and heartache, and there will be times of fun and joy. It is my sincere hope that you will find one idea that will make a difference for that one special child who, like my son, is facing an uphill climb.

1

FACING THE FACTS

On a beautiful December afternoon, I delivered my middle son, whom we called JD. The hospital staff was buzzing with excitement. Just about everyone had picked a date and time for this milestone birth. Now the staff was eager to find out who had won the contest to determine which baby was the five-thousandth to be born that year. It was our son. The hospital had been hoping to reach this magical number before year-end and now a new record had just been set. As a result, three hours after JD was born, local television cameras arrived on the scene to feature him on the evening news. How special was that! It wasn't until later that my husband and I found out just how special he was.

JD's first year seemed to be very much like our first child's, though I did notice that he did not fall asleep easily in my arms as many newborn babies do. Looking back, he was the only one of the three children that would rather be put in his crib to fall asleep than to be rocked. As JD was approaching his first birthday, I was just a little skeptical that he was not saying "mama" or "dada" and he really didn't verbalize much of anything. However, when we went to his one-year check up, the pediatrician said everything seemed fairly normal other than he might be slightly behind in his language development. He assured me not to worry; after all he was just a year old.

When he didn't seem to advance by the age of two, however, I began to worry. JD could repeat a word or two, but he was not really using language as a means of communicating. At his two-year check up I remember embellishing what JD could say, but yet was internally questioning what was normal. I asked myself when a child should be verbalizing and talking. To ease my mind I looked at a book or two on the subject. I did not want to admit that his development, for some reason, just did not seem right. In comparison, my first child talked in full sentences at 15 months. However, I was informed that my first child was very advanced and that I should not compare the two children.

As the next few months passed by, friends and other family members always had a suggestion or two about JD. It seemed as though he did not like to interact with others and was happy to be left alone. In addition, JD did not play with the normal things that my older son did, yet seemed fixated on certain books or objects. My son appeared to be developing unusual fears, did not use the English language, would only eat about five different foods and seemingly was becoming more and more frustrated with himself and others. Noisy places also bothered him and figuring out what it was that he wanted was getting difficult. All the while my husband and I made excuses and went on like nothing was wrong. But inside it was becoming more and more apparent that JD's development was not what the textbooks defined as normal.

In my heart I knew that JD was very bright. It was just that his development was not normal. When JD was three, my third son was born. While caring for a new infant was challenging in itself, it was also time to do something for my middle child. Here I was with three children, ages five, three and newborn and I did not have time or know what to do. I also had a 15-year-old stepson who lived with us and was a big part of our family. He was into a host of sports and teenage activities. I worked full-time and my husband's career was keeping him from home many hours each day. My husband was sure that there was nothing wrong with JD. As far as he could tell, he seemed to just do things a little differently and if we had patience he would develop in his own time.

I did not agree.

The pediatrician had not offered any suggestions, mainly because I was not giving him the full story on JD's development. It was like I did not want him to know. Somehow I was at a loss to discuss his situation with anyone. Even though I considered myself to be an educated individual, I did not know what type of doctor to call for an evaluation. Looking back on it, to be honest, I did not want to ask. Finally, one of my aunts, who lived across the country and was in the education field, subtly suggested that I could have him tested through our local school system. But I did not have a clue who or where to call and I did not think the information she gave me was correct. However, I decided to call the local schools and, sure enough, after the age of three the school would give JD a set of developmental tests free of charge.

This was the beginning of what I labeled as my "make the call anyway" method of operation. I made up my mind then that no matter how ridiculous my thoughts or actions might seem, or where they might lead me, I would follow them for the love of my son.

Parents, this is lesson number one. Do something sooner rather than later. Do not wait. It may not seem right, but do it anyway. Follow your gut feelings. You can always wipe the egg off your face later or try a different path. But begin doing something for your child right away.

The school tested JD and this marked the beginning of our journey. It was June when he was tested by the local elementary school speech pathologist. I remember it was not easy, as JD wanted no part of this person and had no concept what was happening. It took quite some time and I did not want to hear the outcome of the tests. When she brought JD back to me we sat down for a few minutes and I remember her telling me that she still needed to compile the test results, but that she was sure his development was nowhere near that of a three-and-a-half-year-old and that we would need to take action immediately. I wanted to cry. Inside I began asking the big questions of "why me?" and "why him?" My heart was broken in a million pieces and it hurt so badly I could hardly drive the few miles home. Heartsick was not even close to describing how I felt. I was devastated before even knowing the full results of the tests.

When my husband arrived home, I immediately told him about the testing session. He reacted by saying, "I don't think anything is wrong with him. He will be fine. This stranger does not know him. I don't believe it." It seemed as though the anger had set in and he did not want to face the fact that our son had an issue, let alone that he might have some neurological disorder. Denial was the safety net that we had hidden behind up to this point. I came out from behind that curtain sooner than my husband, but needless to say it did not take very long for him to open the curtain and look at reality.

I am sure many parents have been through this very struggle and some have accepted the facts more quickly than others. It is not easy. The reality is that we are brought up in a society of perfectionism and we would all like life to be perfect. We want the best for our children and for life just to fall in place. But it doesn't always happen that way. Realizing that your child does not have all the stars lined up in a row can seem like the end of the world. This is an extremely difficult time for many families. Others may try to empathize with you, but unless they have been slapped with the same reality check they just can't know how you feel.

Like everyone else, you have to get up in the morning and put one foot in front of the other, but now you have to face the fact that your child has a learning disorder. If you're currently facing this situation, define your fight and make the commitment here and now to do whatever you can to make a difference in your child's life. Realization is the beginning. The future of your child will take hard work, time, commitment, and a never-give-up attitude. As I kissed my son goodnight, I promised that we would take this journey together.

REMEMBER

- Do something—the sooner the better.
- Remember realization is the beginning.
- Do not be afraid.
- Ask your pediatrician, a friend or relative where to start.
- Check with your local school system because they will run preliminary tests on your child (generally free of charge) and give you some direction.
- Define your fight and make a commitment to your child!
- Follow your gut feelings.

RESOURCES

Child Development Institute
(www.childdevelopmentinfo.com/development)

Individuals With Disabilities Act (IDEA) (http://idea.ed.gov/)

Ages and Stages Questionnaires (ASQ-3) by Jane Squires, PhD, and Diane Bricker, PhD

Ages and Stages (http://agessandstages.com/)

National Institute of Mental Health (www.nimh.nih.gov)
[search Autism Spectrum Disorders]

Note to Reader: After each chapter are resources that were not available to me at the time JD was in school. I've added them to help those involved in raising or teaching a child with autism or other learning disorders.

2

A PLACE TO START

Once the tests results were in I was advised that JD should immediately begin an extensive speech therapy program. He could repeat a few words, but still did not verbalize in the normal way. If I asked him to say "hello to Grandma," he would repeat, "say hello to Grandma." The report indicated that his motor development appeared to be near his age level, but his socialization and language skills were not much over that of a one-year-old. A complete diagnosis was not really given. The school could assist in free speech therapy, however that was only during the school year, and as luck would have it, the summer break had just begun. Instead the school gave me a short list of names and phone numbers for private speech pathologists in the area. Fortunately, our insurance would cover a major percentage of this therapy. I was also advised it might be good to have an audiologist check his hearing. However, to me it seemed apparent that JD's hearing was fine—though selective.

By now both my husband and I had now accepted the fact that we were in for a very long journey. For us, giving up was not an option. Whatever it took, our son was going to be the best he could be and it was our job to get him there. Now the question was, what was the best that he could be? We decided we wanted him to be happy and succeed in life so we set the sky as the limit. The reports from his early tests did not look very promising. We were told JD would never test well in school or in anything for that matter. As parents we should not expect too much. In the meantime I had made up my mind that the tests were just a series of tests—nothing more. I did not want to believe the results. But at that moment I decided to do whatever it took to help my son. JD deserved every opportunity to overcome his shortcomings. After all, we all have shortcomings in one way or another. JD's had just been pointed out on paper.

Since speech therapy had been recommended, that is where we began. The speech pathologist at the local school system recommended a few names. After researching each one I chose a speech pathologist that worked out of her home. I knew a hospital or office environment would just cause more anxiety and fear for JD. Since I had no knowledge of speech therapy, I did not know what to expect. As we approached the pathologist's workshop I remember my nervous system being stretched to its capacity.

Deb, our new speech pathologist, met us at the door of her therapy workshop—which was a large colorful room attached to her home. Naturally, JD did not want to get out of the car. With considerable coaxing, I finally got him out of the car, carried him into the workshop room, and the work began. After just a few minutes of discussing the therapy process, Deb informed me that I would not be in the room during these sessions. Instead, she said I could watch from an adjacent room through one-way glass which was in the window of the door that led to the adjoining room. As Deb quickly escorted me out, JD cried and banged on the door. He just wanted his Mommy. It took all I had to stay put and not enter the room. I just wanted to pick up my crying, head-banging child and take him home to a safe environment. Though he could not see me, I could see and hear him. My heart still breaks to think of the fear and pain he went through that morning. Deb picked up my son and took him to the other side of the room and he would come right back to the door that I had gone through. Believe me when I say it was very hard, but because of the love for my son and the love in my heart, I had to give it a chance.

Our appointments were at 8:30 a.m., so I could take him to speech therapy, get him home and then go on to work. After a couple of sessions like the first one, JD began to settle down and the learning began for all of us. Though I initially hated that one-way glass, after a few sessions it actually became the beginning of how I would learn to help my son. Initially it forced me to watch him cry and suffer. Then, as he became acclimated to the sessions, it allowed me to observe Deb's teaching methods. I watched how she worked with JD and the sessions seemed very helpful.

Still, I was not convinced that I was going to be able to handle this added responsibility. After all, I had a job and needed to work. It would be far from easy. Work was 60 miles from home (120 miles round trip, five days a week) and it was a challenge just to find the extra time to get JD to speech therapy. Even though I drove a long distance to work, I was fortunate that my hours were flexible. This allowed me to be there when my family needed me. I decided to give it a try.

Everything I did turned into education for JD. I will forever be indebted to Deb as she pointed me in the right direction. Every learning session that JD had with Deb, I would reinforce at home. When I set the table for dinner, folded the laundry, gave him a bath, changed his younger brother's diapers, went down the stairs or back up the stairs, I tried to engage JD in some form of learning experience. It seemed as though the times that we actually sat down for a one-on-one learning experience were few and far between. My goal was a half hour three times a week, but that rarely happened. I just worked the learning into our normal routine.

At first, Deb worked on colors and then moved quickly to letters. The therapy had only gone on a little over three weeks when, to my husband's and my surprise, JD began verbalizing all of his colors and distinguishing his entire upper and lower case alphabet. He was, after all, only three-and-a-half. The speech therapy and what I called "fast pace home therapy" were proving to be worthwhile! The learning did not always go so fast, but obviously we were encouraged by his progress. When you asked JD to show what color orange or blue was, he would point out that color. He could point out a letter of the alphabet when asked and, on occasion, even verbalize some of the alphabet. As I thought about it, I really believed that JD already knew the colors most children knew by his age. He just did not know how to verbalize them. The alphabet was a sheer bonus as we got our big boost of encouragement early on. We thanked the guy upstairs for that because it would have been so easy to give up. Do not ever give up!

Each time we traveled to Deb's we took the same path, which took us past three farms. As we drove by, I would point and say, "cow." I did this going and coming home for weeks. Then one day JD verbalized the word cow and associated it with the animal. I was delighted. We moved on to the horse and the pig.

JD was visual so as I set the table, I showed him the fork over the table and showed him the fork under the table. I repeated this until he understood what the word over and under meant. Anything visual was great. However, try teaching a child who is learning strictly by visual aids the concept of "if", as in "If *this* happens, then *that* will happen." Abstract meanings were very difficult. Many lessons over the years took time—in some cases lots and lots of time and effort. But we never gave up. It was important to remember the saying "when the going gets tough, the tough get going."

Deb started a book for JD with pictures of himself. I learned to use pictures to ease his fears and teach him new experiences. I wish I had known about this tool a year earlier when he was two-and-a-half. JD had stood up then quickly sat back down in the bathtub because he was upset that I had taken the water out of the tub. When he sat down, he hit his head on the edge of the tub, which split his chin wide open. My husband and I rushed him to the emergency room, as we knew he would need stitches.

He was frantic and scared of the emergency room surroundings and the doctor. I tried to quickly brief the doctor about his fears. He didn't listen; of course he knew more than I did. When the doctor bent down to take a look at his chin, he said, "Let me look at your chin. You're such a nice little boy." Just then JD clocked the doctor's head with his foot, sending his glasses flying. My husband and I were about ready to die as the doctor's glasses hit the wall on the opposite side of the room. Needless to say JD had to be put under anesthesia to get a few stitches since there was no other way to ease his fears. We had to hold JD down so the nurses could give the shot that would sedate him.

JD had many unusual fears. But when he was scared, there was no calming him down. Fear seemed to shut everything down. While many experiences can alarm young children, JD's fear was extreme. You could not communicate with him when he was scared. Reasoning with him was not in the picture. As a result, pictures became our tool. I began showing him pictures before we went places to help ease his fears, especially new experiences or the ones that he had been fearful of in the past. It immediately helped with doctor visits, haircuts, and new environments (like a trip to the zoo). We used photos of him at the zoo to teach the names of the zoo animals. JD loved numbers, letters and sports, so we capitalized on those areas; they would help to hold his attention longer.

When it came to learning the names of the animals, we used sports teams like the Chicago Bulls or the Chicago Bears. Since routine doctor visits usually required two to three nurses to hold him down to get through a checkup, I began asking for five minutes alone with my child in the room. During that time I would visually show him what the doctor was about to do—check his ears, throat, and reflexes. I showed him all of this prior to the doctor entering the room. This seemed to ease his fears and made the visits less stressful for the doctor, JD, and, of course, me.

We used pictures of things or the objects themselves as visual aids to show JD what he could expect. I placed pictures on index cards to help him associate with what I was trying to teach him, or where we were going or what we were going to do. I also used photos to reinforce what he was learning in speech therapy. When I was going to the grocery store, I showed him a picture of the grocery store. When it was time to go home, I gave him the index card with the picture of our house on it. If JD could not or would not be in the photo then we used his brothers or others familiar to him. Everyone in the family was engaged in helping JD.

Deb taught us to set goals for JD. The goals seemed small, but for him, whenever he achieved one, it was a huge accomplishment. When setting goals we used things he liked or he could associate with. He did not do things the same way as most children or even his siblings. I had to customize each learning block and goal to him. Before starting something new I always communicated everything with Deb, and I continued to follow up each lesson she taught with reinforcement at home. It just seemed to keep us on the same page and make the learning process for JD that much more effective.

With the use of visual aids we set up a chart of things we wanted to accomplish along with awards he'd receive for completing them. Each reward that we chose for him was shown visually on the chart. The rewards were a challenge to come up with. JD was not like most children where a tasty morsel would suffice. He wanted no part of a delightful candy treat, nor did he want a toy. Once I remember finding him sleeping with a can of alphabet soup because he fixated on the letters on the label, so we turned items like that into rewards. Other rewards became the case that held the latest video, or an item that related directly to that video. We used anything that he attached himself to as a reward.

I remember trying to get JD to try new food items. This was becoming a necessity, as the list of items that he would eat totaled five. These items were hotdogs (no bun), French fries, macaroni and cheese, peanut butter and jelly sandwiches and fruit snacks. That was it. No ice cream, no candy, no fruit, no vegetables, no meat, and especially nothing that was nutritional.

By the time he was four years old the pediatrician told me to only put the things on the table that I wanted him to eat. He assured me that he would not starve, saying, "He'll eat when he gets hungry enough." Well, after almost two days went by and JD did not eat a thing, I took another direction. His will power was incredible, stronger than mine. Our entire family engaged in trying to help him try other foods. We began trying to imitate JD. I know it sounds funny, but he would sniff everything before he would eat it and if it didn't smell right he would say "No want it." So we all began sniffing our food. Then we would take a tiny taste. After each person tasted the new food item, we would clap and congratulate that person. After several meals, JD would sniff his food as always and pretend to try to taste it so we would congratulate him and encourage him to taste. Each week he would get a little braver and finally he began tasting new foods while we clapped and congratulated him profusely for his effort.

JD was also funny about textures of foods, so if he did not like the taste or the texture we did not make a big deal of it. But for the things he did like, I made a point of serving them more often, along with adding a new item. Mealtime was indeed a family affair and it worked well for us. Although there were times that this did not go as smoothly, especially when JD was in no mood for experimenting, I did not push the issue and we tried again another night.

I would advise everyone to study their child and take notes about their behavior. You need to find out what unlocks the doors in your own situation. What worked for our son may not work for the next child. Watch your child at play, when he is getting dressed, while bathing and eating, when watching TV or any other activity. You will want to watch the expressions and emotions of your child. The approach we took helped me the most since I knew him better than anyone. Then I would think up ideas that might work based on what I observed. I zoned in on his strengths and weaknesses, likes and dislikes. Not every idea worked, but many did, and those that did began to unlock doors and get us to a place were we could unlock another door.

At one point several of our friends and acquaintances were talking about preschool and what their children were doing. We signed JD up for preschool at our local elementary school when he was four-and-a-half. We had signed up our older son at age three, but I was extremely worried with this child. For one, JD was not yet fully potty trained. But I knew that the preschool was only for two hours, three times a week, and I prayed that he would get through it without the teacher finding out. Finally, I did get him potty trained about three quarters of the way through the preschool year. JD also did not talk in full sentences, but I explained to the teacher that he was in speech therapy three times a week and that he was making progress. I knew that the preschool probably wanted to say that my son could not attend, but somehow I convinced them to keep him. JD desperately needed interaction with other children.

While in preschool JD would not use a crayon like the other kids and he did not seem to be learning what the other children were. I remember him getting upset once after I had turned off the television. I wanted him to learn to use a crayon, but he was not going to do it because he wanted to watch TV. Since JD would not use a crayon, as this was one of his many unusual fears, he finally took my hand, put the crayon in it, and directed my hand in a circular motion. When he was done guiding my hand the picture looked like a globe. He kept pointing to the TV saying "La la loose, la la loose." This verbalization was something we had been trying to figure out for quite some time. What was he trying to tell us? He frequently would say "La la loose," and we had no idea what it meant. This time he pointed to the globe that had been drawn, then the television, and kept repeating the syllables. I realized that I had just turned off "La la loose" or *Headline News*. At that time, *Headline News* featured a globe at the beginning and end of the program. The network always ran the sports scores along the bottom of the screen. About a week later, we found out that JD could read at age four-and-a-half. He was reading the ticker tape sports scores. It was a discovery that we just stumbled on to by accident.

We also noticed a problem with JD's hearing. I had taken JD back to the audiologist for the fourth time because it seemed that he did not always hear correctly. Since I was looking for answers, I just kept going back. My gut feeling told me that something just was not right with his hearing. I learned later that it was an auditory processing issue and not a hearing problem. JD covered his ears some of the time, especially when in groups of people or around loud and noisy environments. All I could come up with was that he would need to visit the audiologist again. The audiologist went over the test results with me. She felt that JD had some type of hypersensitive hearing and she fitted him for a set of earplugs that would take the background noise down significantly. The earplugs did the exact opposite of a normal hearing aid that magnified sound. The audiologist explained that he was hearing noise that he could not process from all directions and that he was being overloaded on sound. This explained why he always seemed to cry when he was in groups of people. I felt terrible, as I remember sending him to his room assuming it was the terrible two, three, or four syndromes. He cried at every large family gathering or in places with a great deal of noise. From the tests, I learned that this was merely his reaction since he could not tell me when a noisy environment bothered him. The noise level was just too much.

As we continued our conversation at the audiologist's, much to our surprise, JD verbally began to read the credentials that hung on the wall of her office. Though he could not talk in full sentences at four-and-a-half years of age, he could read. The audiologist asked if I would be willing to meet a colleague of hers, someone who might be able to help. She put me in touch with a woman who specialized in hyperlexia, which, today, many in the medical field place this disorder under the umbrella of autism. That speech pathologist put JD through a series of tests, which convinced us that his disability was hyperlexia. The speech pathologist believed she could help JD. She also gave me a book to read written by a parent of a hyperlexic child. I read the book in three hours then turned to my husband and said, "This is our child"

I had been searching for answers. I had been told that JD was a mystery child and that he did not exactly fit the standard mold of an autistic child. This was at a time—18 years ago—before the autism spectrum was as well defined as it is today. Back then I could not find anyone who even knew the term hyperlexia. The pediatrician did not know nor had Deb, our speech therapist, heard about this disorder. No one that I had come in contact with, except this new speech pathologist, knew of this term. Every specialist that had met my son agreed that he had a learning disability of some kind, but they could not put their finger on the exact problem.

The new speech pathologist, whom I will call Maggie, typically worked with children between the ages of 10 and 16. Most of these children had gone undiagnosed. They were frustrated and had many behavioral issues. Maggie was involved in a special program in a school system that was not in our area. She was extremely interested in working with my child because she had not experienced working with a child this young with hyperlexia. The timing of meeting Maggie could not have been better as Deb, who had become my mental strengthening coach, had informed me that when summer came she would be making a career change. She would no longer be working as a speech pathologist and would not be able to work with JD. In the meantime I had just received very discouraging news on JD's progress at preschool, especially in the area of social issues. I did not know which way to turn. Thankfully, Maggie agreed to meet halfway between her office and our house, since she was so far north of our home. Maggie worked with JD for approximately four months and it was truly a blessing. Maggie had found the password that unlocked our son.

REMEMBER

- Help your child be the best he or she can be.
- Figure out a plan or a place to start.
- Make the learning experience a part of your daily routine.
- Study your child; learn as much about your child as you can.
- Use pictures as a teaching tool.
- Set goals and make a chart of what you want to accomplish no matter how small.
- Do not give up; never, never give up!

RESOURCES

The Hope Institute (www.thehopeinstitute.us)

About.com – Learning Disabilities and Autism Spectrum Disorder (http:/learningdisabilities.about.com)

National Autism Association (www.nationalautismassociation.org)

Center for Speech and Language Disorder (www.csld.org)

Reading Too Soon, by Susan Martins Miller

Kids in the Syndrome Mix, by Martin L. Kutscher, MD

Parenting Science – Preschool Social Skills (www.parentingscience.com)

3

GETTING READY FOR SCHOOL

After being contacted by JD's preschool teacher with discouraging news, a meeting was held in May, prior to Maggie beginning her sessions with JD. The report had informed me that JD was not ready for kindergarten in the coming fall. In September, he would be five years and eight months and I could not believe that he was not going to be able to start kindergarten with others his age.

I felt like someone had just hit me between the eyes with a baseball bat, especially since I had felt that he was making great progress. While I knew he did not speak in complete sentences, he was bright and could read. In addition, JD had begun to draw with a crayon and would sit for hours drawing the logos and spelling the names of the NBA basketball teams correctly. It was amazing. Over and over he would spell the Chicago Bulls, Sacramento Kings, Utah Jazz, Orlando Magic, Cleveland Cavaliers and list would go on for all twenty-seven NBA basketball teams.

He would also fixate on the exit signs on the highway. At home he would draw the exit signs on the computer and then label them with the exit name and number just like he saw them when we traveled. The cities and street names were all spelled correctly. Everywhere we went, he drew an exit sign or a series of signs. Once, on a family vacation to Florida, my husband was at a meeting and I had taken the kids to one of the amusement parks in Orlando. I had the three kids in the car and had no idea what exit to take to get back to the rental home where we were staying. Around the Disney World area, there were several exits to choose from. As I was talking out loud to myself, my older son who was seven at that time, said, "Ask JD, he knows all the exits." In my frustration I thought to myself "Sure, ask my five-year-old-son with a learning disability what exit to take." Despite my doubt, I did ask him, and he blurted out, "23C." Since I had no clue where to turn, did not have a cell phone or GPS system, I decided to take a chance and follow his directions. I took exit 23C and, guess what? JD was right. To this day, you can ask him what the exit number is for various places that he has been to and he can tell you the exit number and name.

I wanted JD to go to school like the other children his age. The school informed me that he did not socialize well and his language ability was nowhere near where it needed to be. After the meeting I rushed to the car and began to cry. Then I cried all the way home and for the next two hours—and on and off for the next two days. My heart ached so badly for my child. I was not willing to accept the school's opinion. While I knew JD needed continued help, I still felt he could handle kindergarten. Even though I knew the school did not know the term hyperlexia, they were the experts on school-age children and it was their job to make decisions. But I did not completely agree with their opinion nor did I feel that they knew my child.

In place of kindergarten, the school recommended that JD attend a pre-primary impaired program (PPI). But by observing him I knew that JD was a visual learner and that he would most likely model the behavior that he saw.

Maggie had also confirmed this for me. PPI was not for him, and I was not about to let that happen. I knew to follow my gut instincts, especially when it came to my son. JD's language tests indicated the verbal ability of about a two-and-a-half-year-old and that he did not socialize well with others his age. Yet he could read and spell, and his computer skills were advanced for his age.

After some investigating, my husband and I enrolled him in a Montessori school, which would fulfill the kindergarten requirement in our state. It provided more of a "Learn at your own pace" environment. Later, after careful consideration, our local school district decided they would create a kindergarten classroom for thirteen children who were all considered developmentally behind and at a learning risk. Fortunately, like us, there were other children in the school district who did not fit the standards for the regular kindergarten. As a result, the school district developed a special class for this group of children and agreed to allow JD to attend. Since he had already signed up for the Montessori school and because we wanted to see which school environment fit him best, we elected to have JD attend both schools; the Montessori school in the morning and the local elementary kindergarten class for students at risk in the afternoon.

While the Montessori school accepted different learning styles, we were concerned that JD would be labeled as having a learning disability in the public school. As a parent it is very difficult to come to grips with the fact that your child will forever be labeled as having a learning deficiency within the public school system. I did not want him to carry a label that said my child was not born perfect. But I had to get past those feelings so that JD could continue to learn and grow.

An interesting aspect of the public school system is the Individual Educational Plan or more commonly known as an IEP. This is like a road map that sets goals for the school year through a set of perimeters that determines an individual child's needs that will be abided to by the school system. The IEP is mandated by the government for children with learning disabilities.

JD needed preferential seating and noise reduction. It was imperative that he not be seated near distracting children. JD required visual instruction and the teacher needed to check for his understanding. To voice JD's special issues required a meeting that was made up of the teachers, school officials and other individuals who would be involved with my child. The initial IEP included the principal of the elementary school, the school speech pathologist, the kindergarten teacher and, of course, my husband and me. We elected to also have Maggie attend the meeting; after all, she was the expert on hyperlexia who had worked with JD for the previous four months. Our fear was that no one in the school system had a clue or even knew the term hyperlexia. During the meeting Maggie trained them all on JD's learning style and disability and my husband and I also provided input. This allowed the IEP to be formatted. At that meeting I provided the school with three copies of a book written about a hyperlexic child. Before giving them the books, I went through each and underlined the parts that pertained to my child. I then asked those in the meeting to read the book so they would have an understanding of my son's disability.

When the summer ended, Maggie had completed her time with JD and was ready to go back to her regular teaching job. To continue his therapy, JD was set to work with the public school speech pathologist. In addition, my husband and I decided to continue private therapy with yet another pathologist. JD would now have two new speech pathologists in addition to his school experience. Once the school year began, JD had Montessori in the morning and the public school during the afternoon. It was, in essence, double kindergarten.

As it turned out, it was to be one of the best things we did for our son because he experienced two different learning styles, which helped him to learn how to deal with transition and change. It was good for him since JD had always resisted change, making any type of routine change difficult. He wanted sameness and he rebelled against having his routine interrupted. The Montessori school was about 25 minutes from the public elementary school, allowing us just enough time to go from one school to the other before the next class started. On the way to the afternoon class, JD ate his lunch in the car and he had to learn to change gears to adjust to the second (more regimented) class setting. It was very difficult at first and I worried about overloading him. But after monitoring him closely we decided to keep him enrolled in both schools for the entire year.

By now I had learned it was extremely helpful to tell JD what his day would be like in advance. I continued to use visual aids. Many times I wrote things down on paper that he could read, and the kindergarten teacher at the public school put his daily schedule on the blackboard.

One of JD's weaknesses was auditory processing, though his visual learning was strong. Every day he looked at the blackboard so he would know the plan for the day. This helped him to learn directives and thus minimized any anxiety the day might bring.

If his routine was going to change for any reason, I tried to let him know early in the week as well as at the beginning of the day. Any advanced notice that I could give him regarding the things that I knew were going to change helped minimize his stress and frustration. Preparing him for change seemed to be the key. Though I was aware that any changes to his routine were always difficult, there were many that I could not control. If I knew that a substitute teacher would be in class on a particular day, I made him aware. If the school was holding an assembly instead of class, I told him. I asked his teachers to do the same. This process was followed at home as well.

To this day, JD would much rather know his schedule in advance than deal with the unknown. Luckily he has learned to cope with the unknown changes.

There were days that JD handled the changes better than other days. Believe me, there were bad days—some of the worst. Sometimes I'd see someone looking at us as though judging my "unruly child" and me; as if all he needed was swift discipline. I could almost read their minds; I knew they were thinking that I was a bad parent. Some made comments like, "I am glad my child's not like that" and "she needs to do something with him." We learned to minimize these situations by giving advanced notice. I often wanted to say to those who judged us that they would understand if they had any compassion. For those who have not experienced this kind of judgment, it can be physically and emotionally draining.

One thing I learned along the way was that I could not make excuses for my child. My expectation regarding behavior was the same for all my children. JD had to follow all the same family rules. He had to follow each and every one of them, though he may have needed extra help in the process of understanding their importance. By the end of the school year we could see such a change in JD. He experienced two different groups of children, two different learning styles, two different school environments, a double dose of learning and a school year that involved daily transitions. I could not have predicted such a beneficial outcome. By the end of JD's kindergarten year his language skills had advanced to nearly that of a normal kindergarten age child—quite an improvement considering he started with the language ability of a two-and-half-year-old. While JD's social skills were still way behind, we had reached an important goal—JD was ready to enter the first grade!

Looking back now, all I can say is that I followed my gut about what was best for my child. Had I listened to the specialists at the public school and put him in a pre-primary impaired program, I know that JD would not have made the progress he did. Though I do not want to advocate that you not listen to the school or the specialists, ultimately the decisions are yours. To make them, you need to gather all the information to the best of your abilities and base your decisions on your own understanding of the situation. I knew my child better than anyone. Because of that, I followed my gut and my heart. Each day

I did my part to teach him new things and reinforce the things he was learning at school and at the sessions with the different speech pathologists. The best I could do was to learn right along with him.

In summary, during his kindergarten year, JD had made big strides. In part, this is because we thought outside the box. For JD, two kindergarten classes were better than one, not just for learning but also for socialization. JD went forward, not backwards or sideways, which is something that very well might have happened in the pre-primary impaired program. In the process, I had learned more about JD's learning style, which had helped me know how to best help him along the way. A very important lesson for me was that I was making the choices about what was right and wrong for my child. I was learning to say "no" to some suggestions and "yes" to others based on my gut and what I knew was best. It is important not be afraid to stand up and fight for what your child needs and to be ready to support your action, if only to yourself. Follow that path you're on until you feel differently, or another door opens that shows you the way.

REMEMBER

- Determine what educational plan is the best for your child.
- Investigate all your options.
- Lay out an IEP or individual educational plan with the school your child is attending.
- Tell your child in advance about any change to their routine.
- Always follow your gut because you know your child better than anyone.
- Capitalize on your child's strengths.

RESOURCES

Education.com (www.education.com)

About.com (http://specialed.about.com/)

Montessori (www.montessori.edu)

Family Circle (www.family circle.com) or (www.momster.com)

4

THE ELEMENTARY SCHOOL DAYS

JD was about to enter the first grade and would be attending our local small public school. Prior to the school year we again sat down for his IEP. The meeting was usually held just prior to the summer break and included his public school kindergarten teacher, his next year's first grade teacher, the school principal and speech pathologist, along with my husband and myself. The purpose was to set guidelines for the coming year. Copies of the underlined book that had been provided to the school were presented to JD's first grade teacher who was learning about him from his kindergarten teacher and speech pathologist. I had added my input about what I thought were the strengths and weaknesses of his kindergarten year. We covered the Montessori school and we discussed what issues might need extra attention.

JD was fortunate that the school system was small and, due to his special needs, we were able to request and be granted a particular teacher for his first grade year. It certainly never hurts to ask, and if the school does not have the best interest of your child in the forefront maybe it is time to look elsewhere or think of other options. That is why we looked elsewhere and had enrolled JD in the Montessori school. In our case, we were fortunate because our school seemed genuinely concerned. We learned early on that it is important to build a positive relationship with the school system. Being nice to those that need to look out for your child is essential. No matter how stressful things get, it is important not to talk down to them or expect them to do more than they can. Remember that the school has many children to be concerned about and that yours is not the only one.

Throughout JD's education I never expected the school or its educators to be solely responsible for my child's education. After all, nothing really matters but the welfare your child. However, getting on the wrong side of the school system will not help. Plead your child's case and do it as professionally as you can while communicating calmly. Let the school know of your goals for your child. But remember that it is your job, not only the school, to monitor your child's progress. I always explained to the school that our relationship was that of a triangle consisting of the child, parent and school. All three need to do their part to reach the goals you have set.

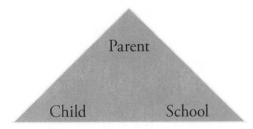

If any one area falls short, the center cannot be whole. I lived by this rule with all my children. The child must do their part, as difficult as that might be. You cannot make excuses because your child has a disability. The goals have to be set high enough so that the child has to reach for it, but not so high that failure is inevitable. The school must do their part as well. The parental role is not an easy one because it requires both overseeing the school and setting the ground rules for the child. It is important for the parent to realize they have the responsibility to continue to help their child through the learning process by reinforcing what the child learns in school. Remember the goal setting that I discussed in an earlier chapter. Things get tougher as video games, computers, television and noncompliance come to the forefront. As hard as it sometimes gets, do not give up. Remember to set your goals high enough and continue to strive to get there. There will be bumps along the road—sometimes they may seem like hills, mountains, and valleys. You will have to be tough and persevere. Remember, the goal is to help your child be the best that they can be.

I mentioned above that you need to oversee the school and your child. Following this rule, I began going into the classroom to observe my child. I did not get the idea to do this until JD was in the first grade, although starting while he was in kindergarten would have been even better. Before visiting, I discussed my plan with the school principal. Then, prior to my visit, I would usually give his teacher a one- or two-day notice. I also made JD aware that I planned to visit his classroom. Beforehand, I made sure that he understood that he was to do exactly what he usually did in class and that we both needed to follow all the same rules. I was just going to be a student for the day.

At the beginning of each school year I explained to the teacher that I would be making these visits and that my first visit would take place about three weeks into the school year. I explained that I was not there to assist the teacher with other children or tasks, though I would consider that at another time. These visits would strictly be to observe my child. I assured the teacher that I was not there to find fault with their teaching style. My purpose was to observe my child in the learning environment so that I could help both my child and the teacher reach the goals I had set for him.

Because I was quite comfortable with our particular school system, I usually gave plenty of notice. Had I not had that level of comfort, believe me, I would have shown up unannounced (which I still did on an occasion or two). My visits were sometimes for the whole day, sometimes a half a day and sometimes for only an hour. I generally visited at least two to three times a semester. While there I went to the lunchroom, music, the playground or wherever he else he went. I just followed his routine.

When I made these visits I always brought a tablet of paper labeled "JD" and also some of my own work that did not take too much concentration. I wanted to appear busy in order to set everyone at ease in the classroom. In these visits I watched JD as the teacher gave directions, as the furnace clicked on, as the other children talked, and also watched how he reacted to those around him. I observed both what distracted him and what he seemed to be focused on. In addition I watched his facial expressions to check for understanding of what was being taught. I took note of his attention span and watched the other children to try to get some sense of how my child was doing as compared to others in the class; especially those who did not have a learning challenge.

On my tablet I made many notes. I put down JD's strengths and weaknesses. I wrote down his reactions to changes, noises and anything that I could observe that pertained to his school day. Was he sitting in the best position for paying attention? Were there noises and distractions? If so, how they could be minimized.

During my very first visit I noticed that even though JD was in the very first row, he had been positioned next to the furnace and a child who was quite chatty. Even though he had earplugs that took out much of the background noise, I could see that the furnace and the chatty child were distractions for him. While the teacher was not taking note of his auditory processing problems, and because I knew JD best, I could see that this was an issue. I knew by moving him away from both the furnace registers and that particular child, he would be more likely to focus and learn. Since the IEP had these accommodations listed, I took advantage of them and asked the teacher to have JD relocated to another seat. Though some teachers are very much in tune to the IEP, others need you to help them understand how it relates to your child.

I already had a collection of notes, pictures, and the like in a notebook. This is something I would encourage every parent to do. Keep a daily journal to look back on. It is a way to measure progress, a reminder for what should be put in next year's IEP, a memory of the good and the bad times and a reminder of what has been successful and what has not. I learned so many things by observing my son. While I knew that he had auditory issues, my visits helped me understand more about his problem. Even though his routine and daily schedule was written on the blackboard, which worked well in the kindergarten year, he did not do well with auditory directives. This continued on throughout JD's schooling, including his high school years. In fact, many teachers told me that what they did for JD was, in one way or another, helpful to the other students in the class.

By observing JD, I learned more and more about his auditory processing problem. He would often miss a word, not process it, or process a different word, resulting in a change to the entire directive. While watching JD in the school environment I discovered that it was very easy for him to think he was doing the right thing while, in fact, he was doing the wrong thing. The teacher might say "We will begin doing your math work right after lunch." JD only processed "we will begin doing math." Then he would get out his math paper and begin working on it while all the other children were putting their things away and lining up for lunch. Needless to say this would put JD at the end of the line for lunch and fostered a feeling of being last, which was always painful.

I learned several other things. When the teacher needed to check with JD for understanding when verbal directives were given, she also needed to maintain eye contact with him. This was something we needed to put in a future IEP. It was also something I needed to work with him on to help develop his listening skills while observing the behavior of others that were around him. Most importantly, it helped me learn that I needed to help the teacher teach my child.

Did I discover issues that I was not happy with? Absolutely, and it was so lucky that I did. For example, when

JD was in second grade I discovered that his teacher had her own agenda and that she was breaking his IEP. I was furious with this whole situation. Earlier that morning I had been in the classroom for about an hour-and-a-half and had left the room in order to discuss his progress with Shelly, the school speech pathologist. Shelly was a very caring individual, who was very skilled in her profession and who truly wanted the best for JD. I always communicated with her so I could follow through with her recommendations at home. We were always on the same page when it came to JD. I gave her my input and she gave hers back. We were a team.

When I came back to the classroom, there sat my son. The other children had all gone out for recess and he had stayed behind. I sat down next to him. All the while, his teacher was at the back of the room. I asked JD why he wasn't out with the other kids playing on the playground. He explained that he was being punished. Upon further investigation I found that the teacher had a rule that was related to students asking questions. She gave the students an opportunity to ask questions prior to going ahead with the daily assignments. If any student asked a question after she asked, "Are there any more questions?" that student was required to stay in for recess. This was the second grade and my opinion was that this particular rule was about the most counterproductive rule that had ever existed. JD had asked a question after his teacher gave her directive and so there he sat, being punished.

At this point in his development, JD had just begun to ask who, what, when, why, and where questions. Prior to the second grade he had never asked a question. Not one. Here he was being punished instead of being encouraged for his progress. Shelley, along with our other private speech pathologist, and I had worked so hard just to get JD to ask a question—any question. We had worked with him for months on this. Upon hearing of JD's punishment, Shelley, I believe, was appalled. The second grade IEP had stated that the teacher had to check with JD for understanding and meaning with all directives. That obviously was not happening. I would not have known had I not been at school to observe on that day. This was something I could not believe was happening. As mad as I was, I went home to collect my thoughts prior to discussing this with the school principal. The next day when we met, the principal addressed the issue immediately.

Fortunately, we managed to get JD through the rest of the second grade year. This was truly the only year out of thirteen that I felt that the teacher needed a "watch dog," which is what I needed to be. I'm sure many friends heard me rant and rave about this situation, but as far as the school system was concerned I handled it professionally. Remember, it serves no useful purpose to make the school system the enemy.

Most of the times, my classroom visits proved to be very positive for JD. In fact he loved those days when I was with him at school. In addition the teachers and I built good and trusting relationships. I always explained to the teachers that I knew JD better than anyone and that if they had any issues to please call or email me right away. I did not want them to wait until conference time or until an issue was out of control.

Once, JD's teacher called a couple months into the school year. It seemed he was having some minor behavior

problems after lunch. He was not himself and was not focusing or settling into the afternoon schedule. The teacher explained that she did not know what had changed. I
went to school the next week and observed JD on the playground. With my notepad in hand, I stood and watched
from afar. JD did not know I was there. What I saw broke
my heart. This was just the beginning of when other children were finding ways to single him out for being different. As a result, he was not having fun at recess. Then,
when he came in from recess after the lunch break, he
was not letting go of his frustrations. Instead he was still
focusing on the playground and not getting back into the
classroom routine.

After speaking with his teacher, we made the playground attendant more aware of certain issues that were
occurring during recess and how they might intervene. I
always was involved. It was not that I did not trust the
teacher to talk to the playground attendant, but I knew
my child best. I asked that a teacher or playground attendant ask JD what he did on the playground while the
students were lining up to go back into school. This way,
prior to going back into the classroom, JD had a chance to
vent any frustration he had. Most days it was something
simple like how other students would not let him play tag
or about how he got pushed out of the line for the slide.

Other frustrations came when JD was allowed to be
part of the group that played football. We had to work
with JD a little more when it came to the rules of the
game. It wasn't that he did not know them, but he carried
them to the extreme. I had to work with him at home in
order for him to realize that the playground game of football did not have to follow the rules set in the NFL.

Before we knew it, the classroom problem had been
resolved.

REMEMBER

- Request a particular teacher that will best fit your child. It does not hurt to ask.

- Make sure the school fits your child's needs and that the school has the best interest of your child in mind.

- Build a positive relationship with the school system or learning institution.

- It is your job to monitor your child's progress. Use the triangle concept of the parent monitoring the child and the school.

- Observe your child in the learning environment. Visit at least once a semester, two to three times if needed.

- Study your child in the learning environment then help the teacher help your child.

- Start a daily journal or notebook early on. Write the good and the not so good things down. It is a means of measuring progress.

RESOURCES

Education.com (www.education.com/reference/article/different-types-resource-rooms/)

Working the System: How to get the Very Best State Education for Your Child by Francis Gilbert

Great Schools (www.greatschools.org)

Success In Mind (www.success-in-mind.org)

5

SOCIALIZATION AND THE END
OF ELEMENTARY SCHOOL

As the elementary school days were passing by quickly, we saw JD flourish in the classroom. His grades were all A's and his retention of what he had learned was incredible. We were so proud of him; he had surprised us all. A pattern of excellence was beginning when it came to his schoolwork. JD had set goals for himself and he wanted to do his best. Some of the perfectionism or OCD (obsessive-compulsive disorder) genes must have come from my side of the family. His classroom work was at the top of the list. Because JD loved computers, he began creating little projects for school on our computer. The speech pathologists were amazed, as was the entire school staff. After all, JD was the child that we were told should go in to a pre-primary impaired program because he would never test well and that we, as parents, should not expect too much. Now JD was beginning to stand out in academics as one of the top students in his class.

But as the elementary years continued, I began to see another completely different issue develop and come to the forefront. Toward the end of the second grade, I began to notice the social situations that were taking place on the playground. Children began grouping together and there stood my JD all alone. As third grade progressed, JD desperately wanted to be included but did not know how to break into a group of kids. Often he would stand watching the others play basketball from the corner of the playground as he dribbled a basketball he had brought from home. Sometimes the other kids would take his basketball because they forgotten theirs and would leave JD out, saying he could not play. It was so mean. As I observed the hurt on his face, my heart would break into tear-ridden pieces. I would get so angry at a playground full of children that were rejecting my child because he was a little different from what they were taught was the norm. It was so hard on me that I usually had to force myself to go out and observe him on the playground. It would have been far easier to stay inside and discuss his academics with his teacher, speech pathologist or school staff. It was sheer torture to watch the other kids call him names, turn away from him as if he was invisible, and laugh at him as he tried to be included. However, looking on the bright side, how lucky it was to have made the decision to go to school and observe him or I never would have known.

My work schedule did not allow me to be at school very often, so I made it my routine to ask JD every day how the playground went that day. I asked him to tell me what he did each recess and how he felt about the things he did or did not do. This helped open the communication channels so that we, as a family, could help him. Our older son, who did not have recess at the same time, was able to give us his prospective of how kids interacted in school and how he was able to break into groups or activities. Of course, that was not easy to apply to JD's situation since our older son instinctively knew how to interact. JD, unfortunately, did not.

We began to reenact individual incidents that happened to JD on the playground. We included both JD's older and younger brothers so we could role-play and teach JD how to handle that particular situation the next time. The role-plays were sometimes awkward and often funny. The role-playing exercises also helped our other children to more fully understand what their brother faced with his learning disorder. There were times JD would say or do something that embarrassed his siblings, which allowed them to react to him. I can remember role-playing situations to show JD how to react when other kids called him names or when they cut in front of him in line. His brothers helped to show him how to break into a group of kids out on the playground that were planning to play football, baseball or basketball.

We tried whatever we could to help him fit in. I made sure he was dressed in the popular clothes so that he was not singled out as being different in appearance. This sometimes was a challenge because JD did not always want to wear clothes that were in fashion because he viewed things differently. I would describe myself as rather conservative; I could not bring myself to buy him some of the "cool clothes" other kids wore. Thankfully JD's love for sports meant he preferred to wear team style apparel. But by helping him conform to what some of the other kids wore, I knew any issues pertaining to his clothes would be eliminated. I knew that he did not need anything that would make him stand out as being different. In order to help him socialize with his peers, I coached him daily and tried to prepare him for upcoming events.

Another issue involved JD's language skills. He had learned to talk in very proper English but this was not what kids his age did. I tried to get him to look at abstract things to teach him the terminology the other kids were using. Of course, this was with the help of my other children. It was difficult because JD saw everything in black and white terms. He did not understand the gray areas, the jokes or the double meanings.

I also tried to give JD a chance to interact with other children whenever possible. We invited other kids over to play (though some found excuses not to come) and his older brother included him in many activities. These efforts helped JD feel included in one way or another.

Because our family was very sports oriented, JD's love for sports came naturally. In the elementary years, my husband volunteered to help coach the elementary basketball program. This allowed JD to receive the personal attention he needed to advance his socialization as well as making sure he learned to understand the directives given during the basketball sessions. This proved beneficial for JD; since his dad understood him, he knew his frustrations and how to deal with him during these situations. Not only did JD learn basketball skills, but he also learned the socialization skills required to survive on a team. The same went for junior golf and little league baseball. During those times that my husband could not be at practices, I tried my best to be there to diffuse any situation that might occur. Sometimes JD's older brother would go along to make it a family affair. We were a family, we were a team, and the family team worked together to achieve the goals of each member of the team. A great deal of our family team focus was directed toward JD.

I found that socialization skills could be taught to a degree, though this was an area that did not come easy for JD. To accomplish this, our focus with his speech therapy had to change drastically. His language skills had most definitely improved and his classroom work was very successful, but his socialization skills were extremely weak. By the fifth and sixth grade, socialization became the main focus. Socialization issues were written into JD's individual educational plan with the main goal to increase his skills in this area. This had to be worded carefully on the IEP. If it was done incorrectly, the school risked losing the funding as the IEP is supposed to be related to education and not social issues. This was an important lesson for us because school administrations are very conscious about how they need to get their government funding, and rightfully so. We had to be careful that the directives were in line to meet our child's needs and not only the need of the school funding criteria. Fortunately for me, our school explained all this and helped to make it all work for JD and the school.

As JD grew older, he was much more aware that no one called him to come over to their house to play or hang out for an afternoon. It was apparent to him how many birthday parties he was left out of and that others had labeled him as being different. Even though I had thought that my heart had been stepped on before, now the elephants were pulling on and trampling my heartstrings.

As a parent I could not take away his pain, but could only help him and teach him to cope with it. I would have given anything then and now to take the hurtful times away. We have all had moments of rejection, but my child was living with them daily. Once, some of the boys had the nerve to make Friday night sleepover plans in front of him and, of course, he was not invited. There were instances when a girl or two called him a nerd in response to him using the wrong word choice. And, of course, this was usually done in front of him and others. I cannot begin to tell you how many times I fought the tears and tucked them away until later so he did not see me cry. My husband and our other children did the same on many occasions because we all hurt for him. The only thing we could do was communicate with him every day to give him an outlet for the stress. Our daily discussions helped JD gain a better understanding of how to handle various social situations by breaking down his daily events so he could learn the appropriate skill required for each situation. I also feel this routine gave him a way to release tension and frustration.

We dealt with all kinds of socialization situations, and some were tougher than others. We had to teach JD how to communicate with the other teachers that he had for art, gym, social studies and music. These teachers only had him for an hour a day and sometimes only two or three times a week. I remember a gym teacher who had given JD a low mark in the social area. It was her view that he was not getting along with the other children. As I talked to the teacher and she gave me examples of the situations that she was basing her judgment on, it became apparent that she did not have an understanding of JD's IEP. It was my understanding that the school was responsible to make sure all teachers were informed and trained on JD's individual educational plan. I learned that while all his teachers were given the information, some of them did not read it or have an understanding of what his particular educational plan was all about.

At this point, I made an appointment with the gym instructor and brought JD along. We discussed with the instructor the situations that had led her to give him the low mark that I was questioning. JD (with my help) was able to explain his side of the gym class incidents. I was also able to educate her on his disability, on his IEP, and the best way to handle an issue when minor situations arose in her class. Just like with his other teachers, I let her know that if she had an issue she needed to call me since I knew my child better than anyone. This teacher immediately made adjustments such as getting JD's eye contact when she was speaking to him. Changes like this made her more aware of his situation; we were now all working together.

Was it the school system's job to bring all teachers up to speed on my child? Was it the school's job to let any teacher who had contact with my child know about his IEP? Was it the job of the school administration to inform teachers that JD's IEP had changed or that JD was progressing forward or taking steps backward? Was it each teacher's job to know what is in the IEP for each child who had one? Yes, I believed so. I had thought these were their responsibilities. After all, they are the educators. But the reality is that it doesn't always happen the way it is supposed to work. You may need to reach out to the lady who runs the lunch line or the school secretary who monitors schedules.

Ultimately, it is the parent who has to make sure everyone is informed as to the needs of their child. It serves no useful purpose to get mad at a teacher or at the school. After all, JD was my child and I made it my responsibility to be sure that all teachers and related school staff had a good understanding of his learning disability. Remember the triangle concept. The average teacher does not want to deal with a child that does not fit the norm, though they do know that this is part of their job. But working with a child that doesn't fit in makes their job that much harder and socialization is not exactly their area of expertise. Education is their main focus and what they are paid to do. Teachers have a classroom of children and each one has somewhat different learning styles. It is important to realize that anything you can do to help make the education of your child easier for the teacher will ultimately benefit your child.

Teaching your child socialization skills is certainly not an overnight project. We continue to work at it to this day. As his elementary years were coming to a close I knew we would have a whole new set of challenges. JD's sixth grade graduation program was a highlight of those years and made us so proud of what our son had accomplished. He even received several awards. JD had come so far while in elementary school. He began kindergarten with the language skills of a two-and-half-year-old and now, at age 11 at the end of the sixth grade, JD was one of the students to receive recognition for academic excellence. I cherished that night as I knew that we had not only reached, but also had surpassed the elementary school goals we had set. The bar was set high and we reached for the stars. That night my son shined like the brightest star in the sky.

However, I was fearful of the next step. JD would cross the bridge to the middle school soon. He would have several new teachers and change classes throughout the day. Could he continue his success? We did not know what challenges middle school and high school would bring, and as we continued on we knew the bar would be set higher. JD would take on the challenges of reaching out for a new set of stars. As I've mentioned before, do not give up, no matter how hard things may seem (or as bleak as the outlook would appear). Our family would have new goals to set, different benchmarks would be used to measure progress and soon a new set of footprints would be left behind.

REMEMBER

- Continue to observe your child in the learning environment. Observe your child's interaction with others. Observe the playground.

- Open whatever communication you can with your child. Give him an opportunity to vent frustration and say how he feels about any given situation. Each day ask how your child's day went.

- Use role-playing as a means of teaching your child.

- Dress your child appropriately so his or her appearance does not give other children a means to single your child out. Keep in mind the latest fashion trends.

- Try to get involved in extracurricular activities so that your child can participate. Use these to help him gain socialization skills.

- Make sure that all the teachers and school staff are aware of your child's needs.

- Work daily with your child on socialization skills.

- Monitor your child's progress and change your course of therapy as his needs change over time. You may need to add something new or change the focus completely.

RESOURCES

Jessica Kingsley Publisher (www.jkp.com) has numerous books for children of all ages with learning disabilities and autism

Nacol – North American Council For Online Learning (www.nacol.org)

LD Online (www.ldonline.org)

6

THE MIDDLE SCHOOL YEARS

In our small school system, the middle school at the time was defined as the seventh and eighth grades (it has since been changed to also include the sixth grade). The middle school building was connected to the high school, though both groups of students were separated from each other. JD was to have classes that changed every hour, which meant six different teachers per day. Many children are naturally fearful of this schedule, since in elementary school they had one primary teacher. In JD's case it was more difficult since he thrived on routine and sameness. Now several teachers would all need to understand JD's IEP and his particular learning styles and needs. Plus, I no longer had a choice as to which teacher would be the best for him. It meant I could not simplify his day nor did he have recess and the playground to break up his day. These were unfamiliar waters for me. The constant change of adolescent age children and all the emphasis that was placed on socialization was an entire new chapter. With JD's weak socialization skills, I was scared. But I knew I could not give up now.

During the middle school years, children were maturing at all different times, and with those changes came boyfriends and girlfriends, groups and classifications and other changes too numerous to count. There were the boy clicks and girl clicks, cool kids and the nerds, athletes and those who were uncoordinated, smart ones and non-academic types, and the list went on and on. It is tough for any child with hormones starting to kick in to survive, let alone a child with a learning disorder. At this stage in his development the primary characteristic of JD's learning disability was his lack of social skills. His success now was hinging on his social adaptability. At the time I can remember thinking that if we can make it through this, we can make it through anything.

The first thing we did was to call a meeting with all of the teachers that would be working with JD in the upcoming year. Initially I thought about talking to each one individually, but it made more sense to call a meeting with all the teachers at the same time. The meeting included JD's speech pathologist from elementary school, since she had worked with him for several years. We also included the school counselor and the teacher in charge of the special needs children.

The meeting was not run by the school, it was run by me. Of course, I had to have the blessing of the school to make this happen. This meeting was written into JD's IEP, which provided me with the opportunity to hold the meeting. This was an idea that was suggested to me by a close friend who worked within the school system. I started this in seventh grade and these meetings continued through the twelfth grade. These meetings are not to be confused with the IEP meeting, but should be written into your child's IEP. The meeting for the IEP was usually done at the end of each school year to set a plan for the next year. Instead, this meeting was called about three weeks after the new school year had begun. At this point, all of JD's teachers had already had an opportunity to get to know him and had formulated a set of questions and or suggestions. The purpose of the meeting was to put all educators on the same page.

During the meeting I went over the IEP and explained what each marked area meant as it pertained to my child. For example, the IEP might state, "Limit distractions" but that definition might mean something quite different to each person. I made sure that limiting distractions in JD's case meant that he did not do well when seated near or in work a group with a disruptive student. He also should not be near anyone who constantly put down another person just to feel good.

By this time I had learned, by observing JD, what pushed his buttons in a classroom setting and what shut down his learning capabilities. In this meeting I explained to the teachers how JD learned and about his strengths, weaknesses and social skills (or lack thereof). I went through his fears (and my fears) of different situations. I also covered his past, present and goals for the future. This all pertained to my child. If any one teacher could not make the meeting I made an appointment and met with them separately. I knew that this effort would ultimately make their jobs easier.

At the end of the meeting I gave all the teachers my email address and all contact phone numbers so that I could be contacted if they needed any understanding or assistance. It was important to make it easy for them to get in touch with me. I made it very clear that I did not want to have to wait to hear information at a periodic school conference, but that I wanted to immediately hear about any problem areas. It was important for them to understand that any issues needed to be addressed sooner rather than later. All this was imperative to JD's success, since it was challenging to turn around issues or habits of any child, let alone one with a learning disability. If not guided properly, it could take a child with a learning disability three, four or five times longer to recover. I made this very clear and communicated that it was not an option to go down the wrong path.

In addition, I made it known that I was always available to step in, help, and support each teacher in reaching the goals I had set for JD. Then I reiterated the triangle theory of school, parents, and my child, and explained that I would be in class periodically to observe. Though I had started this in seventh grade, in retrospect I really wish that I had also done this in elementary school with gym, art, and various other teachers so that everyone would have been on the same page. A meeting like this gives parents an opportunity to go over their child's IEP. Later on, I questioned whether I needed to do this in the eleventh and twelfth grades since JD was doing so well. But I did it anyway and, as it turned out, I was glad I did.

Each year the meetings seemed to get better. Teachers who previously had JD could explain to the other teachers the things they had tried and what worked or did not work. All the teachers seemed to benefit. His Spanish teacher once told me that most of what she did for him was simple things that usually proved beneficial for most of her students and actually made life easier in her class. For example, when she found out that JD learned best with the use of visual aids she began to put all of the class assignments on the black board. Prior to that she had not felt that high school students required daily assignments to be posted there. However, after she began doing it she discovered that other students also found it beneficial and the constant questions on homework assignments stopped. The Spanish teacher found this so helpful she began selling the idea to other teachers. Success stories like this helped me to establish a network of teachers within the school who supported and helped JD to succeed. This meeting format is something I highly recommend to anyone whose child requires extra help.

I will stress this again: in my opinion, smaller school systems tend to be easier to work with. While larger school systems may have more programs, they can be less flexible. It is up to you to decide what is best for your own child based on their individual needs. While most teachers got on the bus and were very helpful, occasionally I did run across a teacher who just did not care about my child's success. This, perhaps, was because it seemed inconvenient to them or that they were too set in their ways. Teachers who were not adaptable to JD's needs required me to work a little harder with JD in their classes and I had to monitor progress more closely. I remember a situation where the instructor and size of a class were not a good fit for JD. My gut feeling was nagging at me and I knew that this class would not be beneficial for him, so I requested a move from that class to another. Fortunately, the school accommodated my request after I explained my reasons to them in a professional manner. A word of caution: do not do this too quickly because your child needs to learn to deal with all kinds of people—teachers, students and administrators. As JD grew older it became apparent that I could not protect him from everything (as much as I wanted to) and it was important to teach him how to adapt. This, of course, was much easier said than done.

JD's schoolwork was excellent in part because he was blessed with an incredible memory. It was what got him through so many schoolwork assignments. One middle school teacher was fond of giving an essay question for a test. She always gave the essay question the night before so the students could formulate in their minds what they wanted to write when the essay question was presented to them the next day. The essay had to be two pages in length. JD would write down how he was going to answer the essay question. He would review his answer for five to ten minutes and then ask me to listen to see if he got it right. JD would then recite the essay, word for word. The next day he would go in and write the exact response word-for-word, on the test. He would pull an "A" every time. He had learned how to capitalize on the strength of his memory. Though he was never tested, JD exhibited many traits those with photographic memories exhibit. This was something in which most educators, speech pathologists, and others who came in contact with him agreed.

I feel that it is worth repeating that it is important to figure out exactly what your child's strengths are and build on that foundation. JD's memory had always been strong, evidenced by his early memorization of exit signs and NBA teams. This explained why he could read at such a young age. By the middle school years, he had learned how to use this strong asset to achieve academic excellence. I could not have been more pleased with his progress. However, the middle school years were just the tip of the iceberg when it came to the socialization challenges we had yet to face.

REMEMBER

- Call a meeting with all the teachers and staff that will be involved in your child's education. Go over the IEP as it pertains to your child.
- Make sure teachers know that you want to hear about a problem sooner rather than later. You do not want to wait and hear about it at conference time.
- Give the teachers the best and easiest means of communicating with you. Email is great.
- Make it known to all teachers that it is not an option to go down the wrong path. Define the goals for your child.
- Go over the triangle concept each school year.
- Make sure the size of the school and the school system meets your child's needs.
- Build on your child's strengths.

RESOURCES

HelpGuide.org (www.helpguide.org)

Scholastic.com (Starting Middle School) (www.2scholastic.com)

A Parents' Guide to the Middle School Years (by Joe Bruzzese) (www.middleschoolyears.com)

7

SOCIALIZATION
AND THE MIDDLE SCHOOL YEARS

The teacher meeting had taken place and the middle school years were in full swing. The speech therapy that existed at the elementary school was gone since it was decided JD no longer needed assistance with language development. The resource room was now available should my child need extra help. However, I continued to communicate with JD on a daily basis as to how his day went. It was becoming more and more apparent that he was frustrated, hurt, and so badly wanted to fit in. Several young twelve- and thirteen-year-old kids were making themselves feel big, while laughing at JD and making him feel small. Fortunately, his schoolwork was solid and he strived to get all A's. He was trying so hard to fit in and just be liked by the other kids. Once I remember him saying, "If I could have just one good friend that accepted me for me."

JD always wore his emotions on his face and his heart on his shirtsleeves for all the world to see. If he was happy or sad, angry or content, frightened or confused, it was all spelled out with silent communication. The non-verbals told the whole story so JD was easy prey for other middle school children who now considered themselves "cool." They poked fun of him and usually got the best of him. The students who had ego issues used him to make themselves look good. They found ways to embarrass him because he did things a little differently than the norm. These kids usually would put JD down in front their peers. It is hard enough for any child to deal with this type of behavior from schoolmates, let alone one who could not come up with an instant comeback line. Worse yet, when he tried, his word choice was improper or incorrect for the situation. This would only escalate a bad situation.

Girls his own age wanted nothing to do with him. As I mentioned earlier, as a parent you have to be around the school at least occasionally to see things like this. That way you get to know about these real challenges and learn how to try to figure them out in order to help your child. You need to chaperone a dance, be around at sporting events, or work the concession stand so that you are aware.

You cannot force other kids to treat your child right or to get them to understand their disability. Believe me, there are times when you want to fight your child's battles and put the these students in their place. But, that would only make things worse. It is a real feeling of helplessness. The elephant had not let go of my heartstrings and now it seemed as though a herd of them were pulling in unison, trying to pierce my heart.

I remember the middle school dances when not a single girl wanted to dance with JD for fear of being ridiculed by other classmates. I also remember a time when another boy had warned him that if he showed his face at the upcoming dance he would suffer the consequences. Fortunately, his older brother vowed to protect him, which assured me that JD would be safe as he walked home. Evidently, there was a boy who just plain had a dislike for JD. The conflict finally ended, after a second altercation occurred in the school hallway, when both boys were called into the principal's office. Fortunately JD was not at fault and the other boy received an in-school suspension and spent the next three days in the principal's office. The bad news was that this incident only served to isolate JD more as a new group of kids now rejected him. This is one of the downfalls of a small school system. When the entire seventh grade class totals sixty-five students, word travels fast. There are fewer kids to choose from to associate with, or to call on to be friends. On the other hand, a larger school system would have more than just one boy threatening to harm him—maybe even a gang.

The heartache and sadness on JD's face was so apparent and there were many days that I just wanted to break apart. But I could not give up. Little did I know at the time that the hurdles could be worse. Kids in the middle school years can be rude and sassy but most are just trying to figure out who they are. I just could not believe that they could be so mean.

JD was sought out by kids to work with him in a group because he had proven to excel in the classroom. But, at the same time, it was obvious to me that they really did not want to be his friend. Mostly they unloaded much of their schoolwork on him in order to get a good grade. Often JD would complain to me that he had to do all the work and did not understand why.

In the case of other group projects—that were not so time consuming or challenging, or the grade was just a credit or no credit—guess who could not find a group? Well, of course it was JD. There he would sit without a group to work in. If no one felt like they needed his assistance, he could not possibly be part of their group. It always amazed me how the same kids that needed him for last week's tough project did not want anything to do with him on the next one. This was a problem that existed throughout middle school and high school. When no one wanted to work with him, he said it felt like the world was against him.

I recall an incident involving groups of three students in high school. No one wanted JD in their group, so the teacher gave him the two kids that were not there that day. What was the teacher thinking? The two kids that were absent happened to be two kids that ridiculed JD on a regular basis. They skipped school and could not care less about achieving a decent grade. JD did his best on this particular group project, but his grade suffered because of the other two since the grade calculation was determined by the combination of all three students. It was not fair.

Finally I had to express to his teachers that these less intensive group projects were very detrimental to my child. I eventually encouraged teachers to assign him to groups so he would not be left to his one-man group.

As a parent it is important to keep asking questions. Find reasons to go to school, because if you don't you will not know what your child is going through. You cannot help if you do not know what is going on. But be prepared, as this will surely break your heart. As you go to school it is not uncommon to find many things that can make you angry or that you may want to change. Even so, remember that it is easier to work within the framework of the school and not from outside. The outcome will be better for your child if you make friends with the teachers and administrators. If you approach them with respect and with the attitude of working together to help your child, the result will be more favorable. The school system cannot be seen as the enemy. Instead, I am stressing the importance of establishing a good working relationship. Believe me, it is not easy. There were times that I could have walked into the school and made my feelings known in an unprofessional manner. One technique that worked for me was to try not to go to the school when I was angry. I cannot say that I never went to school feeling upset. Luckily, on those rare occasions I brought my husband along to keep me in check.

The group concept mentioned previously was classroom and schoolwork related. However, my main concern was how it was hurting JD's self-esteem and affecting him socially. To him it spelled out in capital letters that he was not liked and did not fit in. We all need to feel that we fit in, especially children in the middle school and high school years. I highly recommend getting your child into any group that can help him feel a part of things and does not hurt his self-confidence.

I always encouraged JD to reach for the stars. To succeed he needed to keep trying. I kept encouraging him to jump the hurdles and join organizations. He was in band and in church groups. We even encouraged community service and school groups.

JD was also involved in sports. He thrived on statistics and loved most sports. Having been brought up in an athletic family, he was very determined. Because he attended a small school where student athletes were at a minimum, he was a member of the seventh grade basketball team. As luck or genes would have it, he was somewhat athletic and his motor skills were good. This was great for JD because he could feel part of a group. Fortunately, he was taller than many boys his age so he received a reasonable amount of playing time. After each basketball game was over, his team was required to watch the older eighth grade team. Occasionally, they were also required to attend and support the female basketball team as well. Unfortunately the social struggles were too frequent. His teammates would always want to sit with others on the bench and JD was often excluded or left sitting alone. As a student it was so not cool to sit with your parents—so he sat alone. I watched the behavior of the other students at all the various events. Often I made it a point to go to the girl's volleyball games or stay for the next game after one of JD's games. It was my way of keeping the details in front of me. At these other events I took notes on how the social interactions went.

Continue to keep a journal. Just like in elementary school, I talked to JD about these social situations. Based on the information that I had written down, our family continued to role-play and help JD learn social skills. In those days I used a camera. Today, with the camera built right into the cell phone, it would be much easier. Many have video capability as well. During events I took snap shots of various students in groups. Using the photos we worked with JD on group dynamics—how to follow the group, be part of the group, and to not always feel that he needed a special invitation to stay with them. Of course there were times that no matter how hard he tried, the world just seemed to come down on him. For example, a mean kid would tell him that they were going down to the other end of the gym but that he was not welcome to join them. JD would sit all alone at the opposite end of the gym. We talked about his feelings at these times and I tried to keep the communication channels open. To help him work these situations out, our role-playing continued within the family.

Once I came up with an idea for a conflict box. I wrapped an old shoebox in colorful paper and applied stickers to the outside and labeled it. The box can be decorated with emotions of happy or sad, or in any way you see fit to meet your child's needs. On slips of paper, JD would write down his feelings, frustrations, bad incidents, things that hurt him or made him angry. One at a time he would put them into the conflict box. Then we would try to make time during our busy week to take one, two, or three slips out of the box and talk about each one. We tried to make it seem like a game each time he pulled one out of the box. Sometimes he would want to throw the chosen one back into the box because he really wanted to find a particular one that reflected what was bothering him most. With each slip, we would go over how he felt, how or what he could have done differently and what he might do in the future given the same set of circumstances. This seemed to help a great deal for a while. JD was putting his anger and frustrations on paper and letting his feelings out rather than bottling them up inside. We were able to discuss the situation and learn from it.

It became more apparent that we had to sit down and talk about social situations daily as JD was very frustrated and hurt. As a parent I could see the immaturity of the other kids, but JD could not. All he knew was that most of the time he was either being made fun of or he was alone and unwanted by his classmates. A new set of social goals had to be made as the future brought with it new challenges for us to face.

REMEMBER

- Communicate daily. Keep asking questions. Find out how and what issues your child is having to deal with.

- You need to be around. Chaperone a dance or go to an event that your child will participate in. Find reasons to visit school.

- It is very hard to be a parent and your heart will ache for your child, but don't give up and do not isolate your child.

- Do not call school when you are angry. You need the school and teachers on your side.

- If your child has socialization issues, get him involved in a school group, church group, club or a sport.

- Write down notes on the school or the social activities you attend.

- Continue to role-play.

- Take pictures of social interactions and use them as a teaching tool.

- Start a conflict box.

- Continue to keep a journal.

RESOURCES

Model Me Kids (www.modelmekids.com)

Social Skills Training (http://socialskillstraining.org)

Bullying Statistics (www.bullyingstatistics.org)

8

SUMMER CAMP AND ACTIVITIES

The summer months were times that I also kept JD busy, sometimes in surprising ways. My goals during the summer were twofold: I did not want him to slide backwards, and I wanted to give him every opportunity to continue to grow and move forward. Both the private speech pathologist and the school pathologist took the summers off. When we dropped off our older son at summer basketball and outdoor camps, we usually went as a family. JD also had expressed an interest and seemed to want to attend a summer camp. This prompted me to think long and hard as to whether or not to sign JD up for any camp. What would happen at an overnight camp when I was not there to solve his problems?

After a great deal of thought, investigating, and a lot of pure guts, I signed our eight-and-a-half-year-old JD up for a week-long overnight basketball camp that our older son had previously attended.

Three things made this possible: 1. Our older son would be there the same week; 2. JD could room with his brother and his friends; and 3. it was only 40 minutes from home and not far out of my way to work. My older son was eleven at the time and very responsible for his age. He, to whom I am forever grateful, agreed to help out with his younger brother. As a result, JD's first camp experience went well except for one afternoon meltdown when he lost track of his group. Luckily his older brother came to his rescue and helped out with the situation. That week I checked in each morning and went back in the evening to watch both boys play in their nightly basketball games. It was a good way to break JD in for the summer camp scene.

Summer camps also helped keep JD away from computer and video games. Normally he wanted to spend most of his free time on the computer and the electronic world, sometimes for hours and hours, day after day. Camp put him into environments that helped with socialization and transitions. Change was still hard for JD. Getting outside his comfort zone, I believed, would allow him to experience something new. One great thing about summer camp was that the days were on a schedule and there was always a routine to be followed. The campers woke up at a certain time every day, had breakfast, an activity, lunch, rest period, another activity, dinner, an activity, and bedtime. The schedule was the same each day, and for the most part the routine was set. Even though the specific activities changed, the overall daily schedule was mostly the same. This was a big advantage for JD, as he liked routine and sameness. Summer camp forced him to expand his horizons, try new activities, and make some choices on his own. He had to live with other boys and try to get along with others outside his family.

The next camp I sent JD to was a couple of states south of us. My husband had connections with a golf camp, and JD loved playing golf. I had a stop-gap if any major issues occurred. My husband had a good friend who lived not far from the camp and could drive to the course and help out if necessary. Of course, our older son was also attending the same camp. So we took the risk of sending JD. This camp was golf, from sun up to sun down. Since JD would fixate on the things he loved to do, and he liked to do the same thing over and over, this camp worked out great. Just like we did at school, I met the camp counselor that would be assigned to JD, along with the camp director. I provided each with reference pages that pertained to JD, his disability, instructions of how to handle meltdown situations, notes about how to communicate with him (such as eye contact), and the list went on. Now, with the Internet, email is an easy means of communication. Back then we relied on landline telephone service since cell phones were not something everyone carried around (and rarely did a child have one). Luckily, today, communication is so much easier. I just prayed that every day was going smoothly. Golf camp went quite well, however, some difficulties occurred socially. JD did not feel anyone wanted to hang out with him and some of the campers made fun of his word usage. So it was a little frustrating at times.

The next camp was a big one that JD attended for many years. Shock and amazement are words that come to mind when I think about our decision to allow JD to attend a camp in Canada (another country of all places). It was about eight hours from our home and happened to be the same camp I had attended when I was young. Camp Bil-O-Wood in Blind River, Ontario was owned and operated all these years by the same family. It is a camp that encourages children to reach out for his or her potential while working on self-confidence and self-esteem. And yes, JD's older brother attended the camp as well. We had no idea how we were going to figure out the finances for more than one child to attend, but somehow we made it work. There was no way I would have allowed JD to attend this camp without his older brother. After all, he was only ten years old. Another challenge was that the camp only had two sessions, which were either four or eight weeks with nothing in between. Today the camp offers two-week sessions, but that was not the case when my children were young.

The camp was out in the middle of nowhere and it did not have indoor plumbing, which meant the campers had to use outhouses. The cabins were very basic and the kids' housing assignments were based on age groups. This meant JD would be housed separately from his older brother. The thought that my boys could not be in the same cabin was very scary for me as well as for JD. I really do not know how he managed to get through that first four-week session without having his brother in his cabin. Fortunately, the camp did allow a great deal of communication between JD and his older brother. As always, I explicitly went over directives with my older son. To his credit, he was willing to take on a great deal of responsibility and was also committed to helping his younger brother succeed. I provided outlines and reference pages dealing with JD's learning issues. Before the session began I met with several of the camp counselors and went over everything that I could think of that they would need to know about JD. I also stayed the first few days of camp in a local motel. This allowed me to go to the camp and observe JD in this environment. Once I was comfortable with the situation I returned home, leaving JD at camp for four weeks in Canada. Wow! This was a big step for any child, let alone JD. It was also a big step for me as the parent.

As with most kids his age, JD was initially homesick when he was away from home. Bedtime, as always, was an issue. The camp leadership allowed my older son to go to his cabin at bedtime for the first week until JD's routine was established. As it turned out, JD was having a good time. Camp Bil-O-Wood had a big focus on athletics and JD liked to focus on basketball. This was good because my boys were able to do this activity together. The camp attracted children from the ages of eight to approximately seventeen and is co-ed. It sits in the most beautiful surroundings of trees, beautiful rock formations and clear, sparkling waters. Values and friendships were taught as well as how each camper could become the best he or she could be. The camp set forth to accomplish all these things by using the beauty of the Canadian wilderness. Older campers were expected to help the younger campers and each year the campers were encouraged to reach for a higher goal.

Canoe trips were a big part of this experience and even involved the younger campers who started out with a night or two in the wilderness. Each year campers worked their way up to longer trips, which went deeper into the undeveloped areas of the wilderness. Trips for the older campers were ten to fourteen days in length. In addition to being longer, the rivers and lakes that were paddled became more challenging. The portages—carrying your pack, food and hefting a canoe over your head— each year became more difficult. Some portages were three miles or more for the older and more experienced campers. I could not imagine

JD doing all this, but he did. My child learned to set goals and challenge himself. At his request, in subsequent years, he began attending the camp for eight-week sessions. Each year he worked his way up to a tougher trip as he learned to push himself to the next level.

It remained hard for me to send my children to camp for the summer, especially JD. But at least my children were together and I was able to visit three times or so each summer. This camp was not just fantastic for JD; it was for all our children.

With all of the great experiences, there was also the down side—the not so great part. JD's social issues did not disappear. There was always one kid who was mean and outspoken in the group or cabin who would make fun of JD when the counselor was not around. Also there were all the same adolescent issues that he had experienced at school. JD was always the kid who seemed to be the target; the lost coat, the missing fishing pole, even a CD player—items never to be found or returned. It frustrated him to no end, but I always explained that this was the real world and he had to learn to cope with these issues. But it was not always easy.

Just like in school, one year JD had a terrible counselor that did not understand him or want to help him. That particular summer was rough. I had to intervene and talk to the camp director to help with the situation. JD did write letters home and I could talk to him once a week on the one and only camp telephone. While this did not seem to be enough, somehow we made it work.

Camp was just another stepping stone or learning block. This camp shaped all of our children, but it especially helped JD to learn to deal with others. The experience helped him to deal with situations on his own without my constant supervision. I remember the camp director telling me numerous times that "mothering could be smothering." Nonetheless, I found it very hard to let go, and though the camp experience was harder for JD than our other children, he survived. He learned valuable lessons that have helped him along the way and he will carry these experiences with him always.

REMEMBER

- Come up with summer activities that will help your child to grow and continue to move forward.

- Getting your child outside their comfort zone may help your child to expand his or her horizons.

- Summer camps usually have a routine that is followed which can be a benefit to your child.

- Finding the right camp or summer activity is imperative to your child's experience. Maybe start with just a day camp.

- Do not be afraid to call the camp and discuss your child's situation and learning disability to see if the camp can meet your child's needs. Ask about what disabilities or learning disorders that the camp has dealt with in the past. Ask the camp for references.

- Do the same things for camp that you do for the school experience. Meet with the camp counselors and directors. Provide written information about your child as it relates to his or her disability. Be detailed.

RESOURCES

Camp Bil-O-Wood (www.bilowood.com)

My Summer Camps.com (www.mysummercamps.com)

Chooseacamp.com (www.choseacamp.com)

Camp Resource.com (www.campresource.com)

9

THE FIRST TWO YEARS OF HIGH SCHOOL

As mentioned previously, the high school that JD was to attend was in the same building as the middle school with each school at opposite ends of the building. JD was very familiar with these surroundings so the change from a building standpoint was not an issue. He knew where the classrooms, lockers, library, gym, band room, cafeteria and so on were located. It was a relief that he did not have to face the stress of learning a new environment along with all the other changes that would face him in high school. His yearly IEP, which we discussed previously, had been done in June prior to summer break.

About three weeks into JD's freshman year, the school counselor and I called the teacher meeting. In the past this approach had proven to work well. During the meeting the current concerns or issues would be discussed. For us, this was still the best way to bring the new teachers up to speed on JD's learning style, his disability and what new hurdles he would have to overcome. The meeting also expressed our goals for the current school year.

JD, through the help of the IEP, had learned that he needed to ask for help with his schoolwork when it was needed. He was very self-sufficient and this year had set a goal of earning all A's. Since his social life was not great, he always put a great deal of effort into projects and academics. Most of his projects were over the top. It was apparent that he had become a perfectionist. Most of the time it was a good thing though it presented challenges when perfection could not be attained. To his classmates, perfection and detail gave them reasons to believe he was different.

The high school years for any parent and child are always a challenge and I feared our biggest challenges were yet to come. I had a child with a learning disability, a disorder associated directly with socialization. How was my son to relate to others and how was I to figure out what was normal teenage behavior? Teenage behavior is in itself confusing, let alone the issues and particulars of a socialization disorder. JD did not want to be singled out by having his mother showing up to hold his hand and helping him to solve his problems. During high school, my presence would only make his social issues worse.

Early into JD's freshman year it dawned on me that he was learning to exist in the real world and most likely would be able to attend college. For him to do this we had to start letting go. My husband was much better at this than I was, which turned out to be so helpful in helping me along the way. Each day I continued to communicate with JD, asking him about the normal events of the day. I continued to find reasons to stop in at the school. Our older son, who was a senior, was a big help and could be my eyes within the school without me needing to maintain such a constant presence. Sometimes that was a challenge because our older son saw things as most teenagers would and was sometimes frustrated by his younger brother's behavior. It was hard for him to understand why JD did things the way he did and did not get with the "cool" program at times.

Somehow, with help, I stayed in tune with what was going on at school. At this point I volunteered here and there, but my work schedule did not allow for much. I came up with reasons so I could legitimately be around and continued to keep the communication lines open with JD by encouraging him to talk to me about the social issues he faced. It was important to understand how he was feeling. I had opened those communication doors when he was really young and, as a result, JD was willing to share the various situations that were going on around him. He knew I was always there to help and how much I cared. In addition, he also knew his Dad and brothers cared and were always there to help him gain socialization skills. JD may not have been blessed with an abundance of social skills, but he surely was aware of how rejection by his peers felt. Though the arrows of rejection pierced my heart, as a parent it was my job to help him learn how to cope and deal with the heartache that followed.

Athletics seemed to be his saving grace. He was a member of the golf and basketball teams. Because JD had become somewhat of a perfectionist, he worked just as hard at sports as he did on his schoolwork. His work ethic really amazed us. The golf season was in the fall. JD wanted so much to make the varsity golf team as a freshman so he could play with his older brother who was in his final year. JD had set his sights high, but this goal was not easily attainable. Throughout the tryouts I tried to help him understand that this goal may just not be within his reach. Though he did not make the varsity golf team that year, he was able to secure a spot on the junior varsity team. This is another nod toward a small school, as qualifying for a sports team is usually more attainable in a school with fewer students.

Because JD pushed so hard mentally, he almost quit the golf team during his freshman year. In fact he actually tried to quit. Three times during the golf season, JV players were given the opportunity to challenge the weakest player on the varsity squad. If the JV player scored lower, he would move up to the varsity team. JD wanted to play at that higher level so badly but with each challenge, his eighteen-hole score just seemed to grow. The mental pressure he had placed on himself was just too much and he became tense and frustrated. After the last challenge day, the pressure and stress finally did him in resulting in a display of improper sportsmanship. JD walked off the golf course and vowed never to go back. Because I knew of his love of the game of golf, I could not believe that he told the coach, "I quit!" Only after things settled down was I was able to communicate with him. After some reflection and encouragement he called the coach, apologized, and accepted his position on the junior varsity team for the remainder of the season.

Fortunately, prior to the beginning of the golf season I had discussed JD's disability with the golf coach. Because he had gained an understanding of his temperament and issues, he allowed him to come back to the team. After all the pressure of making the varsity team was behind him, JD finished his freshman year of golf. He played well and put up some very respectable scores.

Golf, of course, is such a mental sport and JD did not always exhibit the proper attitude. He wanted perfection and when a shot did not go where he anticipated, or when he was playing poorly, his temperament issues were visibly apparent. One could look at him and know how he was playing as his non-verbal communication told the whole story. Once, I decided to bring the video camera along to a few of the golf matches. I was not looking for the great shot, but instead used it as a teaching tool. Whenever he had a bad golf episode, as I called it, I used the video camera to tape his behavior. I also videotaped other players in his group who were exhibiting good sportsmanship and setting a good example. Then, after the match, I asked JD to view the video. We viewed examples of good behavior and discussed how it related to JD's poor behavior. The very next golf match my son's behavior began to improve, and it continued to get better with time and experience.

Because JD was such a visual learner, I wished that I had thought of using the video camera sooner since it proved to be such a great teaching device. During his earlier grades I used many visuals—still photos, magazines, drawings—but I had not used the video camera as a method of teaching until his freshman year of high school. I found the video camera to be a wonderful visual aid. It provides the means to communicate the message and allows one to review it over and over when needed. It is an easy way to get a point across when dealing with behavioral situations. My recommendation would be to use some type of camera early and on a regular basis. Today, toy manufacturers make cameras that even a young child can use and create a video film to be viewed on a television.

JD still had his social issues and they did not disappear during his time on the golf team. During a golf match, one is usually paired with two or three other players, each from a different school. These players would snicker from time to time as he did things a little differently, and a little extreme. For example, he carried a set of colored markers in his golf bag. At the end of each hole the markers came out and he marked his scorecard, which was color-coded. This allowed him to look at it at a glance so he could tell how many greens he hit in regulation, how many putts he had, how many birdies and bogeys were recorded and the like. Other players looked at this as not normal and viewed him as a little weird.

In addition to golf, JD loved basketball. As a freshman he was moved up to the junior varsity team. The coach was a very encouraging person, which was great for his self-esteem. JD earned a starting position on the JV team and seemed to do really well on the court, resulting in his freshman basketball season proceeding without a hitch. Prior to the start of the season, I made it a point to have a discussion with the basketball coach regarding my son's background. This was something I faithfully did with all new activities as it gave those dealing with him an understanding of who my son was and how far he had come.

As JD prepared to enter his sophomore year, our family experienced a major change. My husband had taken a job about four hours north of our home necessitated by a lack of opportunities in his field near our home. Because JD was doing so well in our school system and was within his comfort zone, at this point we did not want to uproot him from his local environment. We made the decision to keep our children in their school. Though I was still commuting an hour to and from my job, I had the flexibility to stay involved in the daily lives of our children—which was real important to our family. On weekends, either the kids and I would travel north or my husband would come home. As a family we would just have to make it work.

However things had definitely changed and the challenges would be many. My eldest son had graduated from high school the previous June, which left JD without the security of having his older brother in his school. I began leaning on my youngest child for help since I was feeling like a single parent during the week. JD's golf game continued to improve and he made the varsity golf team. I tried to attend as many golf matches as I could. The season went well and he was growing as a person.

Once golf ended, JD looked forward to his sophomore year of basketball. Just like in golf, he made the varsity team as well. However, unlike his JV coach who had built his self-esteem, the varsity coach was a guy who thought put downs and giving the silent treatment would somehow improve him as a player. Nothing could have been further from the truth. Even though JD was a starting player, the mental challenge of keeping that position was more than he could handle. If I had known better, I would have kept him on the JV team. What started out as a great opportunity turned into mental turmoil. With each game, his time on the court diminished and his starting position was taken away. He went from being in a key position at the beginning of the season to not playing even one second in the district basketball tournament. It seemed as though everything that had been gained in the self-esteem department had been put in reverse. At the end of the season, JD vowed to quit playing basketball (however he eventually changed his mind prior to his junior year). As a family we had numerous discussions with him about what he could control, how to react to the coach, and what he could do to change his own attitude.

JD's older brother had played for the same coach for four years and was now playing college basketball. He understood what his brother was experiencing and was able to provide an impact on JD in dealing with the sport. I will, again, stress that JD would have probably gained more during his sophomore year had he stayed on the junior varsity team. However, other valuable lessons were learned as a result of the experience. Personally, I struggled within watching him struggle outwardly. It was another heartache we could have done without. For JD, who liked all his ducks in a row, change was getting easier. My concern was that he was getting overloaded with his studies, sports and trying to fit in socially. He was also in the marching band, which added to his schedule with practice and performing at most of the football games. Sporting events seemed to be a passion of his, whether playing or as a spectator.

Over the years, my husband and the boys had watched sports on television and on occasion went to the big sporting events whenever possible. JD, with his terrific memory, put it to good use memorizing statistical information on all types of sports, teams and individual players. Then, on demand, he could give out a wealth of information to the amazement of everyone.

JD continued to excel in the classroom and had become a whiz on the computer. He could install programs and analyze computer hardware problems. As with many children his age, he loved computers and video games. However, due to a lack of other students his age inviting him to join in high school get-togethers or parties, JD spent far too much time playing video games and working on the computer. Fortunately, his athletic involvement got him away from those habits. It was through sports practices, golf matches, basketball games and the marching band where JD socialized.

He attended homecoming dances and other social events alone and generally came home early feeling frustrated and hurt. There were times that I sat up for several hours talking with him about his feelings. It was extremely difficult to hear about how hurt and rejected he felt. JD's older and younger brothers were very social and he so much wanted to be like them. Fortunately the boys were best friends—something that continues to this day. His brothers, for the most part, tried to include him in their activities as he continued working on his social skills. As a family we continued to role-play and talk about each situation. We also played family board games and joked about some of his incidents. We used these times to help JD release tension and always used humor whenever we could. Humor somehow helped to make the tough times seem a little less stressful. The family board games usually got JD to crack a smile and get away from his feelings of rejection. The games also helped to get him away from the video games and computer. It bothered me at times to see him spend hour after hour, zoned in on his electronic equipment.

Though there were many frustrating times, my overall feeling was that JD was gaining on his disability and socialization. He had overcome the educational challenges as they related to his learning disability. By the end of his sophomore year, we seemingly were making headway with his social skills. Finally I was thinking that maybe I could relax a bit. Little did I know that JD's junior year would turn into a nightmare.

REMEMBER

- Ask daily about social situations.

- Stop in school often to keep abreast with what is going on as it relates to your child.

- Have an older sibling, relative, or a friend's child try to be your eyes and ears at school.

- Go over your child's disability or disorder with coaches or group leaders.

- Use the video camera as a learning and teaching tool.

- Include humor to help get your points across or to release tension and frustration.

- Work on self-confidence and self-esteem.
  This is extremely important especially during the teenage years.

RESOURCES

The Choices Game (http://thechoicesgame.com)

isafe, Inc. (Internet Saftey Education) (www.isafe.org)

10

A JUNIOR YEAR OF UPS AND DOWNS

JD's junior year sprang into action. The high school golf team was off and running and once again he was on the varsity squad where he was proving to be a real value to the team. This was great for his self-esteem. The team was playing well and the high school golf coach, who was a good friend, understood our son. The golf season was moving forward and before we knew it, we were heading for the regional tournament. It was at the regional tournament where we had controversy.

JD, with his incredible memory, knew every rule of golf. One of the rules was that once a player finished their round they could not go back out on the golf course for any reason. JD saw most things as either black or white. There was no gray area for him. A couple of players from another school went back out on the course to watch their teammates and JD noticed them. He reported the players to the golf monitor who had been following his group. This caused a huge problem because the rule called for disqualification, which took that team out of the state finals and put JD's team in a better position. Naturally this made JD the bad guy for reporting the incident. To him the rules are the rules, which he believed in with all his heart and soul. It turned out that one of the players on the other team was the son of a classmate of mine from high school. It made me feel terrible that an old classmate's son was disqualified from his last high school tournament and the state finals.

I could never figure out why, but for some reason it seemed as though a black cloud followed JD. He was a good kid and so undeserving of many of the things that came his way. I can remember so many situations when recognition was deserved but, somehow in error, his name was left off the list. This group or that group would forget to call his name. Once, while in camp, there was an award called "the aquatic expert." JD had worked very hard and had met the requirements. All of the campers who completed the specific criteria where called up front at the year-end banquet, except for JD. While he did receive his award later that evening, the recognition was lost and it was not the same. There were other times his name was left out of the local newspaper for all As or other achievements.

However, this time the fallen team wanted JD's name in bold print. The situation led to the newspaper inquiring who had turned in the players. A derogatory press article was not something JD needed to experience so I did all I could to keep him out of the paper. Fortunately, by being proactive, the golf coach and I were able to keep his name out of the newspaper. After all, JD had not done anything wrong. The other team had broken the rules, but of course, not everyone saw it that way.

The golf team qualified for the high school state finals. JD played steadily in his rounds at the state tournament, even though he did not think so. Because he was a perfectionist, no matter what score he achieved, it was not good enough. All the players scored well and they eventually won the state finals. There we were cheering, congratulating and taking pictures of the team and of our son who was part of the state championship golf team. This was the school's first championship. Never in its history had our school won a state title in any sport. JD was experiencing it all and the excitement was overwhelming. That evening when the team arrived back at the school, the local fire department was waiting with fire trucks in the school parking lot. The team climbed on top of one of the trucks and was paraded downtown with horns honking and sirens blaring. It was an incredible experience and so much fun to have been a part of it all. I can't remember ever seeing JD smile so much. I was as proud as a parent could be and happy that he was going through such a fabulous experience. The team had achieved perfection.

After the parade, the fire trucks returned to the high school to unload the team. There were six team members and JD was one of them. However, I overheard the others making plans to continue the victory celebration without inviting JD. It was mean and it made my heart feel like it was busting out of my chest in pain. JD was unaware about what was going on. I picked up the pieces of my heart off the parking lot pavement and asked another team member if my son could be included. Fortunately, he did not tell me "no," so I informed JD of the plan. He ended up staying at one of the boy's homes and having a great time. It was just another example of how I still needed to step in and help make things happen for him. I learned to keep my ears and eyes wide open to be sure JD had every opportunity. He would have been devastated and hurt had he found out later that the state final celebration continued without him. I also doubt if my own emotions could have survived the outcome of the situation.

Golf season was over and basketball season was about to begin. As I mentioned previously, JD had planned to quit playing at the end of his sophomore year. I encouraged him not to give up nor allow the coach's behavior to get into his head. Instead I urged him to start out with a renewed attitude toward his basketball game and the junior season. To his credit JD changed his mind and tried out for the team. He put a great deal of effort and intensity into each practice and before we knew it he was once again selected to be a starter on the team. It was a position he had earned and, for now, he seemed to be one of the coach's favorites. This would make life on the basketball team so much easier. Remember, a year can make a big difference.

Early into the basketball season JD became extremely upset because he had no friends. No one included him in their plans or called him to do anything. He went to school dances alone, which made him frustrated and angry. I decided to have him start seeing a counselor. This helped a little, but looking back, it was the wrong counselor for him. The counselor listened to him and encouraged him to talk about his social issues. But what JD really needed was someone who could help him to work on interpersonal skills and relationships. The family role-playing and discussions were no longer working and my limited knowledge in this area wasn't much help. JD's social skills were not improving, which meant that his social life was not changing. What JD needed was just one good friend who was not a brother. While I had helped him in so many different areas of his development through the years, I was becoming frustrated and at a loss for ideas. The things that had worked in the past were no longer working.

JD's grades continued to be top notch and his achievement of earning all A's had been against all odds. Remember, when he was young we were told that he would never test well and not to expect too much.

The basketball season was drawing closer to the district and regional tournaments. We were extremely busy with six basketball games a week. JD had two high school games, his older brother had two college games and our youngest had two junior high games. Things in our house were definitely a whirlwind. All this while my husband worked four hours away, continually coming and going, while trying to attend as many games as time allowed to stay as involved with the kids as he needed to. This left so much to me. I still had my daily 120-mile round trip commute to and from work. Somehow and some way we made it work. If I could do it, I believe anyone can find extra time to help their child. It is just a matter of priorities.

One evening, JD had been invited to spend the night at a family friend's house that had two boys around his age. He knew these boys well, as our families had been close for many years. The eldest boy was on the basketball team with JD and the other was in his class. He normally was not invited to many parties, but they were our close friends and several of the team members from the basketball squad were invited. JD had spent the night in their home on previous occasions and over the years this family always tried to include him since they knew he struggled socially.

The NBA All-Star game was on that weekend and JD was extremely happy and excited to be included. While he was away, my husband, our youngest son and I went to an evening college basketball game to see our oldest son play. The game was about three hours from home.

When we arrived back home around midnight I noticed there was a message on the answering machine from our friend whose house JD was spending the night at. Her message asked me to call when I got home. I called immediately. This friend knew JD very well and was always very good with him. She was well aware of his learning disability and social issues. When she answered she explained that things had settled down and JD was fine now. There had been an incident where the other kids at the party had supposedly put Ex-Lax in his cookies. Our friend explained the situation and said that things had worked out and she saw no reason why JD could not stay the night. She just wanted me to know what happened. Hindsight is always 20/20 and I did not follow my gut after hanging up the call. Later, I wished I had made him come home even though the hour was late. The next morning, when JD came home, he was really upset. I knew it just by looking at him. He was always easy to read, because his emotions were always there for the world to see. He sat down and proceeded to tell me about the overnight party.

The story went like this. Our dear friend knew JD well and could read his emotions. She figured out that morning that something was really bothering him and took him aside. She feared another incident had occurred similar to the Ex-Lax prank. He reluctantly told her that four or five of the boys at the party had been drinking alcohol and that one of the boys was her oldest son. She called the boys upstairs and questioned them to get at the truth. Once the boys figured out that JD had been the snitch, they were extremely upset with him. As one would imagine, after that discovery, his already non-existent social life took a nosedive into the deepest, darkest waters of a very cold ocean.

It was interesting how everything seemed to be intertwined. Our dearest friends were connected with the school through employment. In trying to do the right thing the athletic director was informed of the incident by our friend and her son. Since the boys had not reached the legal drinking age, alcoholic beverages were against the school's athletic policy. After the earlier golf incident, we did not need this. Two of the boys including her son, who was a senior, were suspended from playing their final basketball games. Two other boys who were also on the basketball team were caught drinking that same weekend at another party (nothing to do with my son). These two incidents put a major cloud over the basketball team and the season outcome.

The blame, of course, was piled onto JD. By 9 a.m. the following Monday after the weekend drinking incident, every teacher and student in the school system had heard about it. They all knew that most of the student body had blamed JD for the suspensions and not the kids who actually took part in the drinking episode. JD toughed out the basketball practice before coming home from school. I arrived home from work to learn virtually every student in the high school was down on him. This, despite that JD and many of his classmates were members of a school organization called the A-Team, which signed a pledge not to drink or do drugs. Instead, many of the group's members were mad at JD and thought he was wrong. Even his Facebook page was plagued with derogatory messages from so-called "friends." These messages came from students who attended our school, surrounding schools and other areas.

I never could have dreamed something like this could happen to any of our children, especially the one who already had so much to deal with in terms of his social skills. I was heartbroken, angry and upset. It all seemed so unfair. Worse, I did not know how to fix it for him. If only he had been blessed with the social skills required to handle this situation. To this day I wonder how my other children would have handled this type of challenge. JD was completely devastated, as was our family.

The incident occurred around the third week of February. The first couple days JD endured kids yelling and swearing at him, calling him names and even threatening him. As for the adults, many teachers, parents, A-Team coordinators and parents praised him for doing the right thing. As his parents we also felt that he was in the right. After all, he hadn't sought to tattle on the other boys, rather he was asked a point blank question and had told the truth.

I could not imagine that things could get worse, but they did. The students at our high school decided that JD was getting too much "undeserved attention" from teachers and adults. In response, the four classes of freshmen, sophomores, juniors and seniors banded together and no one would speak to him. For the next three weeks JD was given the silent treatment by the entire student body. Students sitting in groups during class, within earshot of him, criticized him and purposely made derogatory comments. No one would so much as say "hi" or speak to him in any way. If he raised his hand and participated in class, someone would say something sarcastic under their breath. It was bullying, plain and simple.

To say he felt devastated was an understatement. The only true friends that JD had ever known now wanted nothing to do with him. His already lonely existence had turned into a black hole. I will be forever thankful for my youngest child who came to his defense. Unfortunately, as a result, he also took abuse. He was called names on the way home from school and had to deal with derogatory Facebook comments as well.

We continued taking JD to counseling sessions, but they did not seem to be helping very much. My husband and I were so worried about him that our other children also began to worry. Words cannot describe how bruised and abused our hearts felt. JD's world was crumbling around him. How could people be so cruel? Our child, whose learning disability mostly involved socialization, did not have the skills to defend himself.

JD played the last few basketball games of his junior year. One was a contest with our school rival. The student section of that school held up a sign saying "JD IS A NARK" printed in big, bold letters. Each time he ran to the opposing team's end of the court they held up the sign. This continued for the better part of the first half. Finally the school's athletic director took the sign away. But the damage had been done. Our team, which lacked some of its starters, lost, and JD was made to carry the blame.

On a positive note, thankfully, some of his underclassmates began to talk to him. I believe that they realized how unfair the whole situation had become.

With the end of the season came time for the annual year-end basketball banquet, attended by all team members including the freshman, junior varsity and varsity teams. Parents of the players were also invited. This basketball banquet was held about six weeks after the drinking episode. During that time little had improved in terms of the treatment JD was receiving. At the banquet each parent was to bring a dish to pass. The players were instructed to sit on the upper level of the cafeteria, which was like a stage, and the parents sat on the lower level. At this point a handful of students had begun to talk to JD, though he had finished the basketball season as an outcast on the varsity team. Upon our arrival we observed that JD had sat down with some of the freshman team members. The underclassmen did not seem to object that he had joined them. When the coaches asked the players to proceed to the buffet line, they also asked that the players all sit with their respective teams.

We watched as several players on JD's team cut in front of him and more or less push him to the end of the varsity line. After he filled his plate and made his way back to the upper level, he found that his team had positioned their chairs in such a way that there was no room for him to sit with them. JD sat alone at a table next to his team and ate his dinner. I was overwhelmed and shocked to see my child sitting up on the stage all alone while all the other teams and players sat together. I could not hold back the tears and left the room to cry my eyes out in the restroom. When I finally came back to the table I noticed my husband was also fighting back tears. Neither the athletic director nor any of the coaches made any attempt to correct or change the situation. Instead they seemed completely oblivious. I was about ready to explode and informed my husband of my need to go home. But he convinced me to stay there for our son since it was undoubtedly harder on him than it was on us. Though I could hardly bear to see him like this, he was acting like one strong kid. Twice more I left the room to drain my overflowing tear ducts. The only thing that got me through the banquet was a JV team member named Nick who, toward the end of the meal, finally asked JD to come join him at the junior varsity table. I will forever hold a special place in my heart for Nick who was kind and caring. He saw the wrong in the situation and was an angel on the stage that night.

I start to cry every time I think about how mean and hurtful the other kids were to my child that night. Even though I knew JD better than anyone, it was not rocket science to see how he felt. After all, he was the kid who wore his feelings out there in the open for everyone to see. I've never felt that the school or coaches did this intentionally; they were all just oblivious to what was happening. To this day, my husband and I wonder why we did not take our plates, walk up on that stage and sit down with our son. I suppose at the time we were both in such a state of disbelief that we didn't know what to do. When we took JD home and after more tears were shed by everyone, we discussed the evening and tried to make some sense of it all. It was a lesson to us to always to be there for our child. How could we have known what our child was feeling had we not been there to witness the terrible experience for ourselves?

At this point, I had enough of watching everyone looking the other way. None of the teachers, coaches or administrators were figuring out a way to help solve this problem. I realized that they simply did not understand what effect this whole situation was having on my child. It was time for those in positions of authority to start looking JD's way. That required a push from me. The snickering from the other students, the silent treatment and the long list of derogatory adolescent behavior that was detrimental to my child needed to stop.

Against my advice, JD had tried to resolve the situation for himself. I had asked him not to contact the mother of his two friends, our dear friend, as there was just too much friction at the time. We had been close friends for many years and JD thought that if he could just sit down with his two friends and their mother, the situation would be resolved. It was a good thought. However, by this time too much animosity had occurred on both sides. The mother was to call him that evening and let him know what time would be a good time for a meeting. Not realizing the impact that all this might have on JD, or knowing that he was expecting to have the meeting that night, she never called. At the time I was unaware of what he was trying to set up. Had I known, after all that had happened at school, I would never have allowed JD to go over to their home without me. That night I came home late from work to find JD sitting alone in the dark in the lower level of our home. He was sinking into a deep depression and told me that he just wanted the pain to stop. My husband was back up north working and I was afraid to leave JD alone in fear of what he might do to himself. I immediately informed his counselor, who was very concerned about the enormous amount of anxiety that he was feeling.

The counselor contacted the school system and put them on notice that they needed to intervene during the school day. This meant changing the behavior of the student body as it pertained to JD. I went to each teacher, one-by-one, sometimes with tears running down my cheeks, and explained to them how and what they could do to help the situation. In simple terms, I expressed to each how depressed JD was. In addition I told them that if they wanted students to work in groups, then they needed to hand pick the group carefully. It was emphasized that it was important to watch and zone in on what was happening when JD participated in class. A dismal picture was painted outlining the seriousness of the situation as it pertained to my child. As a mother, I was angry and wanted to turn my broom on turbo charge and ride it around the school. However, the only way to remedy the situation was to ask each teacher for his or her help.

Within our family, my youngest son was brought up to speed about how low and lonely JD felt. He was instructed to see to it that JD was not left alone and to interact with him as much as possible. His brother in college was asked to call him regularly. An appointment was made to have JD's hair styled, highlighted slightly and updated. Sessions at the local tanning salon were booked. New clothes were purchased. My focus was to help do whatever I could think of to boost his self-esteem.

As a result of these efforts, JD noticed an immediate difference during class. Teachers were stopping him in the hall just to say "hi" and ask him how he was doing. Nick, the student I mentioned earlier, told JD that he was taking a neutral stand on the situation and let him know that he was his friend. A few students began commenting on his new hairstyle in a positive way. Over time, the situation improved slightly.

Weeks before, JD had signed up for a four-day Spanish and art group trip to Chicago. My husband and I had to think long and hard about the trip. With what had happened we were very reluctant to let him go even though the trip was prepaid. But JD wanted to go. It was a chance for him to socialize. Also his Spanish teacher, one of the trip's chaperones, was well aware of all that had gone on.

However, I was really worried because a couple of the basketball players that had been benched due to the drinking incident were also going on the trip. But Nick, who was an outstanding kid with a big heart, was also going. The Spanish teacher picked the room assignments and promised me that JD would room with Nick. She also promised that JD would never be left alone. I even thought about going along on the trip. But then I realized by bringing his mom along things would only get worse. He was already being bullied and criticized enough. Eventually, after much thought, my husband and I decided to follow our guts and let JD go on the educational trip.

After they returned from the four-day trip, JD seemed happier. The Spanish teacher called to let me know how everything went. Fortunately, there had not been any incidents with his basketball teammates and JD was treated with respect and courtesy. She told me of how proud she was of my son. Another student who was on the trip also had socialization issues. At one point, when the group was participating in a Spanish dance class, JD saw her sitting alone in the corner. He knew how alone she must have felt and did not want her to feel that way. So he got her involved and helped her participate. As it turned out, it helped them both.

The Spanish trip turned out to be the turning point for JD. He had a great time and the trip seemed to bring him out of his depression. The trip was immediately followed by spring break. The combination of the trip and spring break seemed to make my son a little stronger.

Prior to the whole basketball ordeal, JD began talking to a girl from another school that was about thirty minutes away. At first they talked over the Internet and eventually over the phone. This girl was a couple years younger than him and came from a very nice family background. She was very supportive of him when the students ostracized him at his school. JD really did not want her to know about his learning disability, hyperlexia or his socialization issues. I think he was being very cautious about what he said and how he acted. By this point JD was very aware that he did things differently than most kids his age.

Once I remember sitting around the kitchen table as a family. I had made the decision that JD, who was approaching seventeen, needed to have a full understanding of his learning disability. This was not our first conversation about the subject, but on this occasion I was on a mission to be sure that he was going to face this issue head on. He was old enough to understand his learning disorder completely.

I started by explaining hyperlexia, which he already knew about, but this time the discussion was with more detail as it related to his learning and social disability. Then I tried to explain why he was struggling socially. As a family we talked to him about when he first started school and was unable to talk in full sentences. We also talked about how proud we were of what he had accomplished so far in his life. During our talk I will never forget the hurt in his eyes as he looked up at me and asked, "Why me, why was I born this way?" I explained that I did not have the answer. Then I related what he was going through to his younger brother who had been diagnosed with juvenile diabetes just the year before. As a family we discussed our attributes and deficiencies. I encouraged JD to research his disability and learn what he could in order to help him understand more about himself.

JD decided to ask the girl from the nearby school to go with him to his junior prom. She accepted, but her parents had one stipulation; they wanted them to double date with another couple. At this point a few kids had begun to talk to JD at school. However, no one was going to go out on a limb and double date with him after the whole basketball episode. I decided to let JD try to work through this on his own. But finally I decided to call the girl's parents and explain why he could not find anyone who would go on a double date. After hearing the story they agreed to let their daughter go to the prom anyway. Then, about ten days before prom, another classmate decided that he and his girlfriend would like to go out to dinner with JD and his date. I was both grateful and delighted for my child. He had a date, friends to go with and was going to his junior prom. I still remember how handsome JD looked in his tuxedo. After all the depression and sadness he had experienced, it was good to see how happy he was that night.

The junior year finally ended. It seemed like it would never come to a close, but we had gotten through it. When classes ended, JD went up north for the summer to work at the golf course where my husband was employed. JD had a job and he could work on his own golf game and spend time with his family in a different town and environment. The summer was going along nicely. JD was signed up to play in several junior golf tournaments and was doing very well. He seemed sure of himself, was gaining self-confidence and we noticed that he was beginning to believe in himself.

Unfortunately, while up north, the girlfriend that had gone to prom with him broke off the relationship. Initially, I thought that JD would be completely devastated, but instead I saw a newfound strength in him. He was learning how to cope with life. As much as I would have liked to have taken away his junior year of high school, it turned out to be the best and the worst year of his life thus far. JD will always remember the state golf championship just the same as he will remember being the school outcast. He learned more life lessons that year than I could ever have imagined. There was joy, there was depression and there were tears and more tears. Through all these experiences, in the end there was a new person who had grown from it all.

REMEMBER

- You can only control what you can control.

- Always be there for your child.

- Encourage your child to continue and never give up. Remember that you cannot give up either.

- Try another avenue if you are not meeting your goals. You may need to change the goals or regroup.

- Do not be afraid to try counseling or another means of therapy. You must recognize the seriousness of the situation and act on it.

- Be open and honest with educators, counselors, doctors or any one that can help you help your child. In particular, go to his or her teachers individually (if you can) and tell them how they can help.

- In bad times, think of ways to boost your child's self esteem.

- When your child is mature enough, sit down and explain in detail his or her learning disorder. Encourage your child to research and learn more about their disability.

- Most importantly, be there to help your child every step of the way as they learn to cope with the challenges in life. Growing up can be a challenge for everyone, but harder for a child with a learning disability.

RESOURCES

LDA Learning Disabilities Association (www.ldanatl.org)

Physchology Today (The Therapy Directory)
(http://therapists.psychologytoday.com

American Counseling Association (www.counseling.org)

11

LIFE AS A SENIOR

With fall quickly approaching, JD was getting a little anxious. How would his senior year go? Would the other kids still remember what had happened during the last semester of his junior year? How many would still hold it against him? My husband and I encouraged him to just go to school and try to maintain mental toughness. Of course, that was easier said than done, especially for JD. I told him that the ringleaders who caused him trouble during his junior year were the seniors who had graduated and would not be around.

The school year began and he started out his senior year with a newfound confidence. I remember discussing with him that there was no way his senior year could be any worse than his junior year.

We had our annual teacher meeting about three weeks after the school year began. The junior year drama was discussed along with our hopes for JD's senior year. It was hard for me to believe that this was his last year of high school. I heard from a couple teachers who said that they had noticed a difference in my child. One comment was that it seemed like he owned the school that year.

The fall golf season always started before the school year and JD had gotten off to a good start with the team. His hard work over the summer on his golf game had lowered his stroke average. He had also decided he wanted to play golf at the college level, if he qualified. At least he wanted to give it a try. I could not believe we were talking college, let alone talking about college golf. My husband, who was in the golf business, had been talking with college golf coaches. We were evaluating any and all options, but I knew the best thing for JD was a smaller college. He wanted to study computer science, which was a natural for him, and he wanted to play golf. The search for a college was on.

The senior year was quickly in full swing. Students began calling JD for the first time in his life. They called to invite him to join in tailgating parties before the football games. After golf matches and football games, he was asked to socialize with different classmates at their homes. It wasn't that all his social issues had disappeared, because they had not, but JD was learning to interact. Another factor, I'm sure, was that other kids his age were maturing and beginning to accept JD for who he was.

For homecoming he had finally gotten his first date. However once more his date stood him up. He just wanted one date for one homecoming dance in his high school career, but it was not meant to be. Though my heart broke for him, I was so proud about how JD was learning to cope with disappointment. He had experienced more than most. I really could see, as dramatic as it would be for me, that JD could actually handle going away to college. Though he had been to camp in Canada, going away to college without any family to look after him would be a challenge.

The college search continued. The letters from golf coaches were arriving. They had no idea of JD's background or disability and I wasn't going to tell them.

I could not believe that my child had come so far.

Dreams do come true! This was the child who at the age of five, and the onset of starting school, could not talk in full sentences. The school system wanted to place him in a pre-primary impaired program, and the testing indicated he would be way below average. We were advised not to expect too much, nor to expect miracles. Now I was experiencing one right before my eyes. My son would be going off to college and possibly be playing college golf.

JD's senior year continued. The basketball season started and his newfound confidence was displayed on the court. He was so driven and focused, and he gave every play his all. He started each game with confidence and that confidence grew throughout the game. Competing coaches were amazed and many quotes began to appear in the local newspapers saying his determination had made a difference in the outcome of the game. I do not think any of them knew his background or of his learning disabilities. Nor did they know the struggles he had in getting to this point in his life. JD had finally learned to deal with his high school coach and finished the season as the leading scorer. Remember, none of this would have been possible had he been in a larger school district. It was all made possible because of our small school.

Toward the end of the basketball season, JD met a girl who was the cousin of one of his teammates. She attended a nearby school. They began talking and she invited him to her senior prom. JD had already asked another girl to his senior prom. Now he had a dilemma to deal with. But for a child who suffered socially, it was a joy to see him have to deal with such a problem. He was going to two different proms with two different girls. How life had changed in one year. JD had also been in involved in a drama class and had an important part in the school play. There are not words to describe how my husband and I felt about his success.

We had one last hurdle to jump over. One last time my husband and I had to advocate for JD during his high school years. This came about when the school system decided to change the way grades were calculated. Up until this time the school had always allowed more than one valedictorian if the top grade points among the students were the same. JD's grade point thus far had been a 4.0, but due to the new system calculation it would mean lowering his grade point to 3.99. At the end of the previous year, when JD was signing up for his senior class schedule, he had been told how the grade calculations would occur and he elected to take an advanced placement class. At that time he was informed that it would not affect his grade point and could be taken as credit or no credit.

Over the summer, the school board decided to make a change. Though the students were informed about the change, there was inconsistency in the explanation. JD had been told one thing, other students another and the school handbook stated yet another. As a result, the school administration did not know how the changes would affect any student, let alone JD. Even though they did not have the answers, they were trying to change the rules at the end of the game. As you can well imagine, we were upset. My child had come this far after having to work twice as hard due to his learning deficiencies and we were about to have the rug pulled out from under him.

Through a series of phone calls and meetings, my husband and I were able to have the school review these eleventh hour policy changes. Their new policy change would only affect three students that year and JD was one of them. I never determined whether the policy change was intended to eliminate two of the three students vying for top academic honors, and really did not care. My primary motivation was to help my child be the best that he could be. After the policy was reviewed, the school decided that it was unfair to make this change for the senior class, especially since there was no clear understanding of how it would be implemented. Therefore, it was determined that JD would be one of three valedictorians. All three students would keep their perfect 4.0 grade points.

During the graduation ceremony, JD was chosen as one of the students to deliver a speech. He had received numerous scholarships, including one from the Lions Club, one from the PGA of America, different ones from the local educational foundation and one from the university that he wanted to attend. JD also won the very prestigious Koning Award that was voted on by the entire teaching staff. The award was given to a senior student each year that best exemplified leadership, character and integrity throughout their high school years. How proud I was of all my children, as they had each received this award at their graduation ceremonies. JD had certainly earned this award as he had been bullied throughout most of his school years and yet displayed a level of character through it all.

After careful consideration, JD decided to travel out of state to attend a small Division II university where he would be a member of the golf team.

How did we get here? When I say "we" I mean JD, our entire family and myself. It was truly a family affair driven by the determination to help JD be the best he could be.

In the beginning we did not know what path to take. It was like walking through a dark forest and not knowing which way to turn. We were searching for a light or a star to show us the way. Many times I wanted to give up or my heart wanted to stop. How lucky we are that JD's inner strength, combined with our love for him, kept showing us what footsteps to take, what direction to turn and what path to explore.

Today JD still struggles with occasional social issues as he has progressed through college. While he still misses a word here and there, he has come so far. JD's grades have been good, which is not a surprise after how he excelled in high school. He has also been awarded numerous academic and athlete awards while attending college. Although not a total surprise, he began college struggling with his college golf team. His teammates thought he was different and many times he has felt alone. But he persevered and during his senior year of college he moved off campus with three of his golf teammates. Over time they, too, learned to accept JD for who he is. They shared a house and even experienced some minor frustrations. But those frustrations are normal and I have no doubt he will make it on his own.

There have also been struggles with dating and with girls who do not want anything to do with him. But that is probably because he does things a little differently. Socially, he still has a hard time reading non-verbal signs, but he continues to work on them. As a result, I have had many phone calls, some in the middle of the night, asking for help on a particular situation or how to resolve a crisis. My husband, JD's siblings and I have always been there for him. As we continue today, he still needs help and support at times when his disability shows through. Most people, not knowing his background, do not realize that he has the learning disability hyperlexia—which falls under that autism umbrella. We are so happy that JD has truly grown into such a fine, caring and loving young man. During his valedictorian speech he spoke the words that told me that I had to write this book. His words told me that I had to tell his story; words that would give others hope and encouragement to help their child reach for the stars. My story shows how important it is to set the bar high for the love of a child, a child who was not born perfect, but born with a learning disorder or disability. Those words came to me shortly after JD took the stage, greeting a crowded gymnasium assembled for his high school graduation. JD said, "I want to thank my parents, for without them I would not be standing here today; especially my mom who always believed in me and never gave up on me."

Those words will forever and ever be etched on my heart. They are truly the words that made the journey worth every shortfall, worth every heartache, worth every set back, worth every effort, worth every disappointment and truly worth it all. Those words are the footprints of a journey left behind on my heart. The journey is not over. We never know what the future holds. Yet we know there will be new trails to blaze and life challenges that are there for us to overcome.

REMEMBER

IT IS ALL FOR THE LOVE OF YOUR CHILD!

RESOURCES

Landmark College
(A College for students with Learning Disabilities)

College Scholarships, Colleges, and Online Degrees
(http://www.college-scholarships.com) [go to section for colleges
with programs for learning disabled students]

AFTERWORD—JD'S COMMENTS

I am JD and I'd like to share some of my thoughts. It wasn't until the seventh grade that I realized I'd have to learn to make adjustments for the learning and social disabilities that I was diagnosed with at a young age. I remembered asking why I was going to speech therapy and doing other things while none of the other students that I called friends were. After being told about my learning disability, the thing that stuck with me the most was that I was capable of achieving anything I wanted in life if I set my mind to it. Of course, back then it was only about getting straight A's and making the honor roll. The approach that I took to overcome my learning disability was to do whatever it took to pull straight A's in all my classes. If that meant staying in for lunch breaks to get help with something that I did not understand, I did it. If it meant giving up playing video games for the night so I could study, I did it. I remained focused!

In the seventh grade I realized the challenge of dealing with a social disability. I remember the middle school years as being filled with major changes for everyone, including myself. People started to branch off into different things since they were given a tad bit more freedom to do what they wanted. For me, I stuck with what I had done in elementary school most of the time, which was studying hard in class and playing pick-up games of basketball during my lunch hour.

I soon noticed that the other kids started "going out" as they called it. Wouldn't it be cool if I had a girl to "go out" with? When I received my first taste of rejection from a girl, I was crushed. After that experience I thought about my situation and realized that the pretty girls were going out with guys that I had thought of as lazy—the ones who did not put any real effort into their classroom performance. I did not understand and asked my family for their help with this situation. After going through the play-by-play version of my rejection, my mother went into a little more detail regarding my learning and social disability.

For a while, I was in denial and did not want to believe that I was different from so-called "normal classmates." Though I thought I still had friends that were considered popular by the others, my eyes were opened when I realized that I was the only one in my group of kids that I associated with that did not go out with a girl during the eighth grade. I started to believe that I was "different" from the average middle school student. Little did I know that this would not be the toughest challenge I would have to overcome in my lifetime so far.

My high school and college years turned out to be some of the toughest times. Social issues seemed to be encountered every day. I found myself asking the same question over and over again; why are things not changing with me? I have continued working on a solution to that question. In the latter semesters of college I finally came to a few realizations. I discovered that a great deal of what I am feeling is the way I react to people who act like jerks. My mom had explained many times to me that these bad times would not be so bad if I did not react so adversely to them. I really did not want to listen to this and much of this was due to going through adolescence. But now I do have to admit that she was right.

I have learned that if I keep believing in myself, despite what others think of me, they cannot get under my skin and break me down. Therefore, I discovered that others will not change the way they act just to appease me. That has made me realize that it would be in my best interest to only worry about how I feel about myself rather than worry about how others feel about me. I know that no one knows me better than me, well, except maybe my mom. Through all of my social struggles I have gained an inner strength. This has allowed me to withstand adversity better than those who have had an easier road to travel.

My interaction with girls has gotten much better as I compare it to my early days of social interaction. I have more self-confidence and a better understanding of the kind of person that I want to associate with. In the past, I tended to put so much pressure on myself. I used to think that I had something to prove to family and friends. As a result I was attracted to people who were not a great fit for me. I am learning that I just need to be me and let the rest fall into place. The perfect person for me will be there at the right time.

Athletics and sports have always been a major influence on me and that interest has helped me overcome some of my social and learning issues. Sports have given me something to work toward and a group of people that I could relate to as friends. If it were not for sports, I do not know where I would be today. But athletics is just a part of my life.

My family has been the best support group to help me overcome my shortcomings. Through the good times and the bad times, my family has always been there. However, my biggest fan through my journey has been my mom. I appreciate how much she has sacrificed for our family and me. When hard times have arisen and I doubted myself, she has always believed in me and told me to never quit. I will be grateful to her every day of my life. I know that she and my family will always be there to provide a helping hand when I need it the most.

I have accepted the fact that my social disability may never be fully eliminated. Therefore, my main focus is to try to minimize this disability as much as I can. For example, I may have to think about things a little more before I say them. My disability may cause more challenges than others, but I am who I am. It really does not matter if people say the right things naturally or if it takes some time for people to master the skill. In my opinion, communication is communication. Though I cannot report that all this has been "pain free"—in fact many times the pain has been unbearable; there is nothing worse than feeling that you are not accepted and you are rejected as a person—I've found ways to get through the bad times and look forward to each new day.

For parents of children with learning disabilities, I would suggest that you interact with visual representations as much as you can. I remember that I learned a great deal through interactive computer software. It allowed me to explore things and learn while having fun at the same time. I spent many hours on the computer learning about different objects and various subjects. To this day, many of these things still resonate in my mind and it has helped me in my education. My best advice would be to never give up on them. Where would I be if my mom had given up on me? If someone believes in you, then it is easier to believe in yourself and create your own success story. I really believe that with hard work and dedication anyone can be a success.

For those of you who have to go through life in a similar way that I do, know that you are not alone. There are others out there just like you who experience the perils of having a learning disability. Do not feel that you are the only one in the world who is different. There are plenty of us. Remember that you have special qualities that others may wish that they had. Be thankful for what you do have. For me, I was blessed with an inseparable, loving family that has always been there for me. This I feel is more important than being gifted with athletic ability or with a charismatic personality. My main suggestion for others is to protect your dreams and chase them. Set a goal to beat the odds. I graduated from college with a major in computer science and a minor in business. I recently started my own business in software applications and market phone applications for the smart phone. I was just hired by a computer software company and am now relocating to another state.

I am not afraid to face the world knowing that I have a learning disability. If you believe in yourself and keep working hard, your hopes and dreams will be within your reach and it will surely be the beginning of a brand new day.

ABOUT THE AUTHOR

KIMBERLY BELL MOCINI was born in Grand Rapids, Michigan. During her high school years she began working in her family's furniture and appliance business, eventually becoming a partner. Early in her career, while still in her teens, when the microwave oven was first introduced, Kimberly traveled throughout Michigan teaching microwave cooking instruction at a time when the oven was considered to be a complicated appliance. That led to her first foray into publishing, writing a microwave cookbook.

In her mid-twenties, Kimberly enrolled in college while still working full-time in the family business. Within four years she earned a degree in Business Administration from Aquinas College in Grand Rapids, Michigan. She also attended classes at Kendall School of Design and attended a Business Management program at Notre Dame.

Married in her late twenties to David, her husband of 28 years, they have three children. Sports have been very important to their family resulting in traveling great distances, sometimes across the country, so their children could participate in various sporting events.

In between working full-time and raising three kids, Kimberly has volunteered in many school and church activities, sat on parent advisory boards and worked in fundraising for countless clubs, sports teams and school activities from grade school through college. She enjoys music, interior design, sports, and poetry. She also believes in family values and that one should live life with character, integrity and honesty.

Beyond all other activities, Kimberly's greatest accomplishment in life has been raising her children all of whom graduated from high school with top honors including a son who was born with a learning disability.